Carrying On the Mission of Jesus

Carrying On the Mission of Jesus

by

J. Todd Kingrea

CONQUEST PUBLISHERS

Bladensburg, Maryland
www.conquestpublishers.com

Conquest Publishers
A division of Conquest Industries, LLC
P.O. Box 611
Bladensburg, MD 20710-0611
www.conquestpublishers.com

ISBN 13: 978-0-9883809-1-2

Library of Congress Control Number: 2012955603

Printed in the United States of America

Table of Contents

Introduction

Do you ever wonder why today's church is so different from the church we see in the book of Acts?

How did the early church do so much with so little, and we do so little with so much?

How did a dynamic Christian movement become a fixed Christian institution?

If you have ever asked these questions, or others like them, this is the start of a challenging, informative journey to lead you back to the heart of the early church. Every major Christian denomination has suffered ongoing membership decline over the last few decades, and there is no indication this trend will change anytime soon. It will get worse. The world of flannel boards, nuclear families going to Sunday school and worship each week, and the church holding a pre-eminent place in every local community are all gone. We have entered the twenty-first century and brought with us a form of church that continues to follow a failed trajectory.

The New Testament paints a compelling, exciting, *dangerous* picture of the church as God designed it to be. However, the reality that we experience on a regular basis seems a million miles removed. Think about it. The Bible shows us a vigorous gathering of men and women, committed to sharing the good news of Jesus Christ, making a momentous difference in the world around them. Of course, they had problems. Almost all of the letters in the New Testament have instructions or rebuke (sometimes both) to different churches in the first-century world. Yet from what we know of history, these ragtag house churches spread the witness and example of Jesus from one end of the Roman Empire to the other. In doing so, many Christ-followers gave their lives for the sake of the gospel. The early church was Spirit-filled, lay-led, countercultural, always in trouble, and risky.

Compare the early church to the church we are familiar with today. Most of our churches are nowhere near *vigorous*. Sharing the good news of Jesus seems to be only for those we feel are "like us." We have not accomplished much that would be considered 'momentous,' except for the occasional knockdown, drag-out church administration meeting. Few of us truly give our lives for the sake of Jesus and his mission. We are not Spirit-filled, lay-led, countercultural, in trouble, or risky.

Why is this?

Simply, because we have been operating in the wrong model — or structure — of church for 1,800 years.

The New Testament gives us important information about the identity, mission, and purpose of the church. It shows us how the church is designed to function when fully submitted to the lordship of Jesus Christ, and imbued with the power of the Holy Spirit. The church is to be an alternative form of community, revealing to the world a way of living grounded in grace, service, love, and compassion. The church is a movement of God's redeemed people, fulfilling the mission of Jesus. It is the physical presence of Christ on earth and the living incarnation of his love and grace.

Throughout the New Testament we see the church operating with a flattened authority structure. Members were involved in all aspects of the church's life and work. All shared equally in the triumphs and suffering as the church spread across the Mediterranean world.

God's design is for the church to be portable—able to move freely from place to place and culture to culture. It is to be relevant to every cultural context in which it finds itself, allowing Jesus to speak to the indigenous people in ways they can understand and respond to. The church should stand out in the world, serving in humility and generosity as a place that offers a life-giving alternative to the corruption, abuse, and fear that dominate human society.

At this point you may be thinking, "None of that sounds like the church I attend." I know the feeling. The reason we find ourselves yearning for a New Testament expression of church, and living in a completely different reality, is because we have deviated from God's biblical design for the church.

Before you begin the actual devotions and Scripture readings in this book, you will find a brief overview of church history. Please do not bypass this section as something boring or unimportant. If we are to reclaim a New Testament expression of church, it is vital that we understand how we have gotten to the place we are. We can't find our way home again until we know where we are.

A few years ago I was in Ho Chi Minh City in Vietnam. As someone who loves to explore new cities, I left the hotel one evening to walk around and see what I could find.

I went up and down numerous streets, all of which tended to look the same due to the similar stores each held. After a time of walking, browsing, and taking in the rhythms of the city's nightlife, I decided to return to my hotel. Unfortunately, I quickly realized I had gotten turned around and was unsure of my exact location. Many of the street names looked and sounded the same. I had been very careful to notice where I was as I went along, but had nevertheless gotten confused. I didn't panic, because I trusted my sense of direction, and knew that, given time, I could locate something I recognized.

Sure enough, after a few minutes I spotted a street name I remembered. Using it as my reference point, I was able to retrace my steps back to the hotel with no problem. I had to figure out where I was before I could get back to where I wanted to be.

The journey to recapture the spirit, passion, and influence of the early church is the same. The section on church history will provide invaluable insight into how the church has become more ponderous than powerful, more monument than movement.

The church has been following a path established, supported, and promulgated by the Roman emperor Constantine the Great. We are heirs of a church based upon a hierarchy of power and control that began in the final days of the Roman Empire, was solidified during the middle ages, and continues to this very day. As Frank Viola and George Barna highlight throughout their stunning book *Pagan Christianity: Exploring the Roots of Our Church Practices,* much of what we mistakenly assume is the biblical church is anything but. We have inherited forms, structures, beliefs, and practices that have their origins in the civil and religious world of ancient Rome rather than in the Word of God.[1] To find the pure essence of the church for today's desperate world, we need to be bold enough to look closely at what the Bible teaches us about the church, what history teaches us about the church, and where our churches find themselves today. In the process, I believe we will discover that we have, in fact, traded God's marvelous design for one of human construction.

I am not anti-church. I am not anti-tradition. I believe passionately in the mission and purpose of the biblical church in the world. I have a deep desire to see congregations, of every tribe and practice, authentically reflect the image and witness that existed in the first three hundred years of the church's existence. This book is an attempt to help others consider where we are, and where God would have us be, as his ambassadors and emissaries in this world.

This devotional is designed to take you through the entire book of Acts in twelve weeks. It can be done in six weeks by doubling up on the readings. You are asked to read the assigned chapters in Acts, followed by the devotional. You are strongly encouraged to respond and interact with the questions at the end of each section.

Read the assigned chapters as often as possible throughout the week. Don't be content with merely reading it, checking it off your "to-do" list, and moving on to other things. God does

---

1 *Pagan Christianity: Exploring the Roots of Our Church Practices,* Frank Viola and George Barna

his deepest work in us when we submit ourselves to the lordship of Jesus Christ and when we willingly cooperate with the Holy Spirit. Take time to read, meditate, and pray each time you use this devotional.

Begin your Bible reading and devotional time with a brief prayer. God desires for us to know and understand his Word, and one reason he has given the Holy Spirit is to help us do that. You might try praying something like this:

> *Lord and Master, my Jesus, you promised that when the Holy Spirit dwells within me, he will guide me into all truth. In this time now, I surrender myself to the teaching, correction, and revelation of the Holy Spirit as I study your Word. Let me see what I have never seen before. Let me see what I have often seen and overlooked for convenience sake. And through this time together, shape and transform me according to this Word. Amen.*

You may have other prayers you choose to pray. The point is not what words you use, but that you are truly opening your heart, mind, and spirit to encounter Jesus Christ through the Holy Spirit in the Scriptures.

At the end of each section you will find a scripture memory verse. Again, you are encouraged to memorize these verses. Psalm 119:11 says, *I have hidden your word in my heart that I might not sin against you.* The more of God's Word we memorize, the more of it the Holy Spirit can bring to our remembrance when needed, the less likely we are to sin, and the more we are formed into the image of Christ.

Following the memory verse is a closing prayer. You may

choose to pray this prayer only once, or you may pray it daily. Incorporate it into your weekly routine in a fitting manner. Also be sure to pray whenever you finish your Bible reading and devotional study. Ask the Holy Spirit to plant what you have learned deep in your mind and spirit.

This devotional guide will only benefit you to the degree you commit yourself to it. The Holy Spirit will only offer you his power and presence to the degree that you want him. You are beginning a voyage of discovery, adventure, and purpose as you seek God's face and will for your church. You may uncover some things that challenge you and your understanding of the church. Some things may even create some "holy discomfort" with what you have always known or believed about the church. That is fine. Do not be afraid of those moments or questions. Embrace them and allow God to speak to you and take you deeper. His desire is that we are more fully conformed to the image of his Son, and that we mature as members of the body of Christ (Ephesians 4:11-14, Colossians 1:28).

Encourage fellow congregation members to participate with you. Perhaps you may want to arrange a small group gathering each week to read and study the Scriptures and the devotional together? What a wonderful way to imitate and demonstrate the early church!

I pray this book will enhance your spiritual growth, and that as a result, God will begin a revitalization movement within your church. May you be open to the touch of the Holy Spirit, so that you may transform the world outside your doors, and bring glory to God the Father!

Church History 101

Before we begin our exploration of the book of Acts, it's critical that we have a basic understanding of how the church has developed across the centuries, and why we have the structure we do today. The following is only a synopsis. It is not meant to be exhaustive, but merely to give us an idea of why so many churches need to reclaim their New Testament roots.

The history of the church begins in the book of Acts. Following the ascension of Christ, the original eleven disciples, many women and other followers — around 120 in all — were still in Jerusalem (Acts 1:13-15). God sent the promised Holy Spirit upon these believers at Pentecost. Three thousand people responded to Peter's powerful sermon that day and were brought into the church. From that point, all of them began to spread the message of the Messiah.

At the beginning of Acts 8, terrible persecution broke out against the Christians in Jerusalem, and all but a few were forced to flee the city, thus setting in motion the command of Jesus in Acts 1:8 ("...*and you will be my witnesses...in all Judea and Samaria, and to the ends of the earth").* As the apostles began to fan out across the first-century world, they carried the teachings and example of Jesus with them.

The church during this period generally met in homes. When faced with persecution they would also meet in catacombs, caves, or other places to avoid detection by the Roman authorities.

Saul, who would later become Paul, entered the scene in Acts 8-9, and after his dramatic conversion on the Damascus Road, became the greatest advocate, missionary, and theologian of the young Christian movement. Paul began a letter writing campaign to various churches across the Roman world in the mid-50s of the first century. These letters provide us with much of our insight and understanding into the early church.

In today's terminology, the formative stages of the early church would be called a *lay-led* movement. There were no ordained leaders, at least not in the sense that we think of them today. The church in a place like Corinth or Ephesus might have dozens of house churches meeting across the city. Leaders were chosen, usually by Paul or one of his traveling companions, who would oversee the church, protect it from error, guide its mission, and be responsible for its health and growth. These were not paid staff positions, but servant leaders of good character and spiritual conduct.

People in these house gatherings shared a common meal and worshiped together. From what we understand, this consisted of reading letters (from apostles such as Paul, Peter, etc.) if available; sharing the message of the apostles; praying; discipling one another; and singing. As the first century progressed, the original eleven disciples were martyred, and writers such as Mark, Matthew, Luke and John penned the gospel accounts we know today.

The church saw and understood itself to be the living example of what God's kingdom was like. They were God's model community. If we want to get a taste of what life in the kingdom of God is like, we only need to look at the biblical church. Its approach to ethics, love, sacrifice, and service; its understanding of family and marriage; the attitudes about money and wealth; and their passion to share the story of Jesus set it apart from any other human grouping. As they followed the teachings of Jesus, this little sect began to have a significant impact on the world around them.

Just as happened in Acts 8, waves of persecution broke out against the Christians. Different Roman emperors, notably Nero and Domitian, went to extremes to try and stamp out the Christian cult, but with no success. Peter and Paul were both executed under Nero's rule. Despite this, however, house churches continued to multiply.

During the second century, the church found itself continuing to survive against the on-again, off-again persecutions ordered by Roman emperors. In addition, heresies and false teachings such as Arianism, Docetism and Gnosticism began to arise. Most of these controversies centered on the person and work of Jesus. These theological attacks against the Christian faith gave rise to the early church fathers (Origen, Cyprian, Clement, Augustine, etc.) who wrote volumes in defense of the faith, and developing the theology we still affirm today.

The year 312 CE marked a pivotal point in the development of the church. Emperor Constantine defeated his rival at the battle of Milvian Bridge and attributed his victory to the God of the Christians. He began to use the letters *chi* and *rho* (the first two Greek letters in the word 'Christ') and the cross as his symbol in battle. In 313 CE, Constantine issued the Edict of Milan, giving Christians equal rights with all Romans. There is some debate as to exactly when Constantine converted to Christianity, or if he actually did, but during his reign Christianity rose to prominence across the Empire. This time is generally considered to be the beginning of what historians have termed *Christendom*. No longer an outcast religion or a minor movement, Christianity began to grow by leaps and bounds.

By the end of the fifth century, the biblical canon of 66 books was finalized. Various councils had met to formalize creeds and statements of faith, to reject heresies and false teachings, and to establish theological positions on such things as the dual nature of Christ and the essence of Christ.

The church was changing dramatically during this time. Since becoming a fully recognized religion, the church became more entrenched with the civil government. The Empire supported the church financially. Constantine was the first to construct buildings (basilicas) for Christians to meet in, and he had an extraordinary number of them built. He also granted special privileges to the clergy, such as exemption from certain taxes. The church was gifted with land, wealth, and political clout. Christians had access, and were often given, high-ranking political positions.

Instead of having to meet in small groups in houses, the people of God could now meet by the hundreds in extravagant buildings. And since Christianity had assumed such a revered and powerful position, professionals were needed to conduct the affairs of the church. Therefore, a hierarchy of religious leaders was developed and implemented. Priests, cardinals, bishops, archbishops and a pope conducted all the affairs of the church. The ministry—that only a few hundred years before was done by every member of the house church—was now the sole property of the clergy.

At this point in history, the church had two separate branches: the Eastern Orthodox Church and the Roman Catholic Church. The Eastern Orthodox Church recognized the decisions of a few different ecumenical councils than did the Roman Catholic Church. Eastern Orthodoxy remains to this day, following a slightly different variation of the Roman Catholic form.

The Roman Catholic Church grew increasingly more powerful throughout the history of Europe. In some places and times, the Church had more authority than national governments. The separation continued between the clergy and laity, with the clergy handling all aspects of ministry, and the laity—the majority being poor and uneducated—were reduced to the role of mere consumers.

The term *Christendom* came into its own during the middle ages. The majority of Europe was Christianized, often at the point of a sword. It was assumed that if you were born in a Christian nation, you were a Christian, and you were expected to fulfill all obligations to the Church such as confession, Mass, and tithing. Severe penalties could be administered for not doing so. Often the threat of excommunication, purgatory, and hell were used to keep the populace in line. Being a Christian had little to do with a personal relationship with Jesus Christ or with the power of the Holy Spirit at work in one's life. It had everything to do with following the rules set forth by the Church.

One of the darkest periods of church history occurred during this time. The Crusades were a series of religiously sanctioned military campaigns waged by much of Christian Europe, particularly the Franks of France and the Holy Roman Empire. The specific crusades to restore Christian control of the Holy Land were fought over a period of nearly 200 years, between 1095 and 1291. Other campaigns in Spain and Eastern Europe continued into the 15th century. The Crusades were fought mainly against Muslims, although campaigns were also waged against pagan Slavs, Jews, Russian and Greek Orthodox Christians, Mongols, Cathars, Hussites, and political enemies of the popes. One of the most disturbing and horrific was The Children's Crusade in 1212 CE. It was felt that the children could take the Holy Land supernaturally because they were pure in heart. It was a colossal failure and most of them were murdered or sold into slavery.

The Roman Catholic Church continued to consolidate its power and dominion over Europe. The Church grew richer, built more elaborate cathedrals, and decided the laity could not receive the cup during Mass, as they might drop it and spill the precious blood of Christ. The people continued to do as instructed by the clergy, fearful of crossing the Church. The celebration of the Mass continued to be delivered in Latin, despite the fact that the majority of people no longer spoke the language. Monasteries and convents arose across the continent as alternative communities that fostered hospitality, simplicity, and spirituality, but even these were under the direct control of the Church.

As the Middle Ages drew to a close, a Catholic priest and theology professor named Martin Luther came onto the world's stage. He saw firsthand the corruption, avarice, and abuse of power that was commonplace throughout the ecclesiastical ranks of the Church. And he had enough. In 1517 CE, Luther penned a list of complaints he had against the Church and its practices, and called for reform. He took them to his church in Wittenberg, Germany, and nailed them to the door. His "Ninety-Five Theses" was the first public act of the Reformation, a direct and unexpected slap in the face of the Church's elite.

Luther took issue with the sale of *indulgences* — a common Church practice by this time — which required people to pay sums of money to "release" the souls of their deceased loved ones from purgatory. It was the equivalent of buying someone's salvation so they would be spared the torments of hell. Indulgences were also sold as a penance for sin, thus negating any sense of genuine contrition, and reducing the whole matter to that of a financial transaction. The great reformer also took issue with the use of the Latin language for Mass, and campaigned to have the Bible available in languages people could understand. His intention was to get the Bible into the hands of the people so they could read it for themselves instead of having a priest do so for them. Luther also advanced the idea of "the priesthood of all believers," a biblically based concept which says that because Jesus intercedes for us, people did not need a priest to receive their confession and offer absolution. That was taken care of in Christ. Luther also returned to a firm position on justification by faith alone, and not on good works such as prayers, holy pilgrimages, or indulgences.

Luther was excommunicated, had attempts made against his life, and was forced into exile for several years. Not far away, in England, the royalty was also growing tired of Roman rules and domination. In 1534 Henry VIII declared himself "The only supreme head of the Church of England," thus beginning a break from the Roman Catholic Church and establishing the Church of England.

The Protestant Reformation began to sweep across Europe as more and more people rebelled against the abuses of the Roman Catholic Church, which retaliated with their own reform-minded Counter-Reformation. Wars were fought and many lives lost over the years as religious groups vied for power and territory. At this point in history the Church once again split. The Roman Catholic Church continued as it was. The Protestant Reformation released people to pursue their faith with some new rules and new traditions.

But only *some*...

The Protestant churches that arose in the wake of the Reformation still bore striking similarities to their Catholic cousin. An ordained priest or pastor continued to handle all the chores of ministry while the laity remained passive consumers. Bibles were made available in all languages and dialects. Worship was conducted in culturally appropriate languages. The sacraments — seven in number, according to the Catholic Church — were reduced to two: baptism and the Lord's Supper.

Protestant church buildings still resembled those of the

Catholics. The pulpit and altar area was located up front, normally sectioned off by a rail or low wall. The message was still delivered from a pulpit. Choirs continued to be used. The most significant difference was in the *focal point* of the worship space. In the Catholic Church, the focal point of worship was the bread and cup — the body and blood of Christ. In the reformers' churches, the focal point was the Bible. It was normally placed on the altar or a stand at the front, thereby emphasizing its importance. You can still find this in a great many churches today.

As we know, the Protestant branch of Christianity has spawned many offshoots, what we call denominations. These arose mainly over issues of theological interpretation (the sacraments, spiritual gifts, and so on), but also over issues of style and substance (music, the use of symbols and icons). These denominations still "do church" the way it has been done for centuries: a professionally trained pastor/leader handles the chores and responsibilities of the church. The laity in general remains inactive and disengaged. With the exception of the charismatic branches, spiritual gifts are rarely discussed and never used. The main worship service in each church serves as the central point of entry for newcomers. Activities and events are designed to attract nonbelievers to the church building, as has been the case since the days of Constantine.

The form of church that we use and have known all our lives is not based on the New Testament. Rather, it is derived from Constantine's developments as he merged Christianity with the Roman Empire. As a result, in the twenty-first century it becomes increasingly difficult to attract people to our buildings. The concept of Christendom — that one was already a Christian simply because they were born into a Christian nation or family — is gone. We find ourselves doing church in an ancient way that has no resonance or point of connection for pre-Christian people today.

While there is much to cherish and honor from the church's historic past, the form must change if the church is to become relevant, powerful, and world changing once more. The model we have inherited throughout the centuries simply does not work when compared to what we see revealed in Scripture. Any form that continues to perpetuate a clergy/laity split, which emphasizes institutional survival over the biblical mission, or which operates out of human power is doomed to extinction. The hope of the church is the hope of the world, Jesus Christ. He is the Head of the body. The future of the church is intrinsically linked to how willing we are to surrender control back to the Holy Spirit, and to reclaim the essence, passion, and presence of the New Testament church.

The Nature and Purpose of the Church

What exactly *is* the church?

This may seem like a simplistic question. After all, many of us grew up "going to church." When asked about which church we attend, we name the denomination to which we belong or the location of a particular building. For many people, church is synonymous with a place to go and something to do.

However, this is not consistent with the biblical witness. Scripture never associates the church with a location or an activity. The church is the people of God, in any given place and time.

Because we have operated in the wrong model of church for centuries, everyone has come to associate church with a building. But Christians across the world, who do not possess buildings designed for worship, exist as the church. Is a group of thirty-eight people meeting under an umbrella thorn tree in Africa considered a church? Yes, they are. How about a house church, meeting under cover of darkness in a remote province in China? Are those twelve people singing in hushed tones to avoid detection by the authorities a church? Absolutely.

In the early spring of 2004, my wife and I visited Ghana, West Africa, as part of a short-term mission team. One of the main things we did during our visit was conduct medical clinics in several remote villages. One morning, after a three-hour bus ride over some skeptical-looking roads, we arrived in a village. They knew we were coming. Pastor Anthony had made all the arrangements for us ahead of time. As we started setting up tables and unpacking our supplies, the people began to worship. Drums and other indigenous instruments appeared as if from nowhere, and the villagers danced and sang to God's glory. We even took a break from unpacking and setting up to join them. We gathered in a frail-looking building that more closely resembled a picnic shelter in a public park.

Yet we had no doubt we were in the midst of the church. The love, joy, and enthusiasm were contagious. They did not have gold offering plates, stained glass windows (they did not have windows, period!), meeting rooms, padded chairs, or fancy altarpieces. They had none of the material items we associate with church, yet they were the living embodiment of Jesus Christ. The Spirit of God was present, without having a single hymnal or church office in sight. They were the church, in its purest form, without all the physical and material distractions we are surrounded with. What we saw and experienced was an authentic expression of New Testament Christianity.

Christianity has lost much by following the wrong model of church. One of the most devastating has been the shift away from a grassroots, Spirit-led movement to one of professional, centralized institutionalism. We have exchanged God's biblical design for one that consolidates power among a chosen few, promotes inactivity and selfishness among the majority, and seeks its own comfort and preservation above all else.

God established the church to be the ongoing incarnation of Jesus Christ in the world. Through the Holy Spirit, the church—locally and universally—proclaims the good news of Jesus Christ, worships God, administers the sacraments, builds up the faithful, acts as "salt and light" (Matthew 5:13-16) in the world, meets society's needs, and provides an alternative community and way of life. The church includes all those who have gone before, the church triumphant; those in the present time; and all those who will belong in the ages to come.

In Scripture the church is described as...

The body of Christ
Romans 12:4-5
1 Corinthians 10:16-17,
12:12-20, 27
Ephesians 1:22-23, 4:11-13,16
Colossians 1:18

The bride of Christ
Ephesians 5:25-28
Revelation 19:7; 21:9-10

Holy Temple
1 Corinthians 6:19
Ephesians 2:19-21

Flock
Acts 20:28-29
1 Peter 5:2

Notice the organic nature of three of these images. The church is alive and active, changing and adapting, growing and transforming. These terms cannot refer to a building or something we do. They represent the very essence of life.

God's intent for the church can be found plainly in Ephesians 3:10 and Colossians 1:15-23. It is to be the agent through which God in Christ reconciles all things to himself. The church's responsibility is to live differently, serve graciously, and love courageously.

In addition, it is to be a unique, set-apart (sanctified) community. It is to show the world how to live in the kingdom of God (see Matthew chapters 5 - 7), how to present and represent Jesus Christ to the world, and how to live in the world but not be "of the world" (John 17:14). The church is to accomplish what no other person, group, or organization can because it operates in the power of the Holy Spirit. If the things our churches do can be accomplished without any need for God, we are guilty of turning it into just another human organization or institution.

The Head of the church is Jesus Christ (Ephesians 1:22, 4:15, 5:23; Colossians 1:18). Pastors serve to proclaim the gospel, administer the sacraments, maintain the order of the church, and ...*to prepare God's people for works of service, so that the body of Christ may be built up...* (Ephesians 4:12). Pastoral and church staff assists in these functions. Pastors are the spiritual shepherd or leader that God has chosen and called to be over that particular incarnation of the church.

The main role and responsibility of the pastor is found in Ephesians 4:12. On occasion I have been asked what a pastor's job description is. According to many church members, it includes a variety of things such as chairing committee meetings, visiting regularly, putting out fires, and fulfilling all the expectations and demands of the congregation. Biblically, however, it is to teach, train, and equip the congregation to carry out the work of ministry in the world. Until we free our pastors from unrealistic expectations and petty demands on their time, and allow them to focus on their biblical responsibility, our churches will continue to weaken and die.

Another significant loss that comes from operating in the wrong model is how the work of ministry has been relegated to professionals who are expected, or desire, to do everything. Church consultant Bill Easum, in his book *Leadership On the Other Side*, states, "Most of today's laity functions as care takers and givers rather than spiritual leaders — going to endless rounds of meaningless meetings, trying to manage and protect decaying institutions from extinction. Most of today's pastors function as chaplains — going about taking care of people, visiting shut-ins and hospitals, serving communion, and mouthing archaic rituals understood by a decreasing number of people. This shouldn't be. These ministries are important, but they are not the responsibility of the pastor. That's not biblical. These ministries are the responsibility of all the people of God." [2]

The role of the church member is to carry out the tasks and work of the church. This is done by full submission to the lordship of Jesus Christ, by active participation in the life of the church, and by the exercise of spiritual gifts. It is not the pastor's job to do all the work of the church. As I have told congregations from time to time, "It's not *my job* to do *your job* in the church." God will not hold me accountable for how well I carried out your role in the church. He will hold

---

2   *Leadership On the Other Side*, Bill Easum, p. 35

you accountable for that. It is the role of the laity — the church members — to fulfill the majority of tasks of ministry. This is the biblical witness.

As you can see from this brief overview, most churches operate out of a Constantinian/Roman model of doing church, more so than a New Testament model. This helps explain the apathy and lack of involvement among many laity, the overworking and burnout of pastors, and the lack of Holy Spirit power and transformation. If you have ever wondered why the church today is not quite like what we read about in the New Testament, now you have a different perspective to consider.

Week One:

Looking Into the Sky

Read Acts 1 & 2

I love looking at the night sky. I always have ever since I was a child. There is something captivating about all that velvety darkness, punctuated by sparkling points of light. The immensity of it dwarfs me. It is the same sensation I have when standing on a beach, looking out over the ocean. I am so small, almost inconsequential, compared to the expanse of the deep or infinite void of night. Sometimes I need to be reminded just how small I really am in order to remember how much I am really loved by God. As we begin this journey through Acts with a desire to recapture its essence and reality for today, we find the disciples standing around, looking into the sky (1:10). That sounds like a lot of churches these days.

One day while Jesus was among them, the disciples "... *gathered around him and asked him, 'Lord, are you at this time going to restore the kingdom to Israel?'*" They were anticipating and expecting a new, tangible kingdom—a restoration of Israel's historical glory during the years of King David. Despite

Jesus' teachings about the kingdom of God as a spiritual presence and reality, these men remained focused on the original social, political, and religious splendor of former days.

In one sense we should not be too harsh with the disciples. God had told Israel that if she remained faithful to the covenant, God would draw all nations of the world to himself through her (Genesis 12:3; 1 Kings 8:43; Psalm 22:27, 86:9; Isaiah 2:2, 49:6; Jeremiah 3:17). Israel would be God's model community, the perfect expression of God's character, through which all people would come to the knowledge of the LORD. Unfortunately, Israel was not faithful. The covenant between Israel and God was repeatedly cast aside, ignored, or willfully disobeyed. It stands to reason that the disciples were still thinking that the "kingdom of God" which Jesus kept talking about would be a return to Israel's glory days. Only this time they would get it right.

However, that was not what God had in mind. While he still longed to draw all nations to himself (as we will see in Acts 10), it would not be through Israel, but through this new expression of God's people: the church.

It is in the response that Jesus gave to the disciple's question that we find the starting point for our move away from the institutional church and back to a world-changing spiritual movement. *"[Jesus] said to them: 'It is not for you to know the times or dates the Father has set by his own authority. But you will receive power when the Holy Spirit comes on you; and you will be my witnesses in Jerusalem, and in all Judea and Samaria, and to the ends of the earth.'"* In essence Jesus tells them, "Don't focus on what you can't know. Focus on what you will receive, and what you will do as a result."

The day Jesus was taken into heaven the disciples stood there, looking into the sky, concentrating on what had been instead of what would be. They were focused on the wrong things. So are our churches today. How much nostalgia do we have for "the good old days"? How many times have we heard people long for the days when the church was full, thriving, and alive? Much of our conversation looks back to "better days" in the past. Like the disciples, we are looking into the sky, convinced God is going to *restore the kingdom* of our church's best times.

But our focus is not just on past glories. We also spend our time, energy, and resources on things that have no eternal significance. Think about how many church meetings concentrate on the color of paint to be used for a nursery, or whether we should ask a Sunday school class to change rooms, or if the choir should wear robes in the summer. Theologically, consider how much energy and attention is lavished on which millennial view of the end times we should support, or when Jesus will return (despite the plain statements of Jesus in Matthew 24:36 and Mark 13:32). Things of this nature tend to distract us from the more important concerns of sharing the gospel and making disciples. It has been said that we too often "major on the minors." Jesus did not want his early followers to stand around staring at the sky because if they did, they would miss out on what he wanted them to do. While many of our churches have the best of intentions, they would rather focus on lesser things than do the hard work of changing lives. Jesus said *"It is not for you to know..."* There is no sense dwelling in a past that will never come again, nor wasting valuable time on things that distract us from our real mission. To reclaim the New Testament DNA of the early church, our focus must shift from what God *did* to what God is *doing* here and now.

The second part of Jesus' reply was that the early church would receive the Holy Spirit. If we are serious about reclaiming the essence of New Testament faith and action, then we *must* have the power of the Holy Spirit at work in us, among us, and through us. It is not optional. Jesus instructed his disciples to wait for the Holy Spirit to be bestowed; otherwise they would have been trying to carry out the message and mission under their own power. Now we have all been guilty of this at times. We have sought to do God's work in our own power. We may have the best of intentions, but without the indwelling, empowering presence of the Holy Spirit, our efforts will always fall far short of what God desires. If we choose not to let the Spirit move in us, lead us, and transform us—as individuals and as a church—then we are not really disciples. A true follower of Jesus submits himself or herself to the transformation and guidance of the Spirit. We will talk more about the Holy Spirit as we move through Acts.

The last element of Jesus' answer to the disciples' question was that they were to be his witnesses *"in Jerusalem, and in all Judea and Samaria, and to the ends of the earth."* The church remains under the same evangelistic orders today. Our witness must be obvious in Jerusalem, that is, our church and the immediate community around our buildings and homes; in Judea, which would be our county or geographic region; in Samaria, those places where we really do not want to go; and around the world.

Because we have been raised in a Constantinian model

of church, where paid professionals shoulder all the duties of ministry, we have become numb to the command to be Christ's witnesses. We want our pastors, priests, or elders to do all that for us, because after all "That's what we pay them for," as the erroneous thinking goes. But this command to go forth and be witnesses was not solely for clergy. It was—and is—to the entire church. There were no senior pastors, priests, or professional missionaries standing there that day, staring at the sky; just a group of misfits, outcasts, day laborers, accountants, homemakers, and fishermen.

The command of Acts 1:8 will be the foundational verse for our study of the early church: *"But you will receive power when the Holy Spirit comes on you; and you will be my witnesses in Jerusalem, and in all Judea and Samaria, and to the ends of the earth."* We will return to this verse repeatedly to see how the early church responded to it. The Lord still expects his body, the church, to fulfill this commission. Sadly, many churches have abdicated this responsibility. Instead of being the living embodiment of Jesus Christ in the world, churches throughout the West have turned inward, focusing on self-preservation and institutional maintenance. We have been operating within the wrong model instead of the one God reveals to us in the New Testament. But there is hope! The church can return to its biblical roots if we are willing to lay aside the Roman imperial model and recapture the essence of the Acts church.

What are some ways you have seen your church "major on the minors?"

Why do we prefer "looking into the sky" instead of focusing on the commands and mission of Jesus?

How would you describe your church's reliance upon the Holy Spirit? Where do you see a need for more of the Holy Spirit's power in your church? In your life?

What are some ways you can be a witness in Jerusalem (in your church and immediate community)?

What or where is Samaria for you? Where are the places that you are reluctant to go? Who do you see or think of as beneath you or "hopeless?"

In addition to the power and presence of the Holy Spirit, today's churches must reclaim a more intentional emphasis upon prayer. Acts 1:14 says *"They all joined together constantly in **prayer**..."* and again in 1:24, *"Then they **prayed**, 'Lord, you know everyone's heart. Show us which of these two you have chosen...'"* We see it yet again in 2:42: *"They devoted themselves to the apostles' teaching and to fellowship, to the breaking of bread and to **prayer**."*

Nothing happens in the church without prayer. This explains the lifelessness often felt in worship, in the lack of response to outreach activities, and in the indifference among so many congregations. If we do not bathe everything in prayer, we are operating out of our own power, agendas, or best intentions. Most churches fail to experience the fullness of God's magnificent power because there is not enough prayer.

We do not hesitate to pray when someone is diagnosed

with a terminal illness or is preparing for surgery. We ask for ease of pain and for protection when we travel. But how often do we pray for our worship services, our outreach events, or our church leaders? How often do we pray for the visitors we have in worship? Until we fully comprehend the necessity and importance of prayer, and fully commit ourselves to devoting time to prayer, our churches will continue to struggle.

In the first few hundred years of the church's existence, prayer was its lifeblood. They had no luxuries, no buildings, no formal standing in society. They owned no land nor had the ear of important politicians. Everything the early church had and did came through prayer. Compare that with all the material trappings of today's churches, and the faint emphasis upon prayer we have. Upon returning from a mission trip to India, a friend of mine commented on how the church there did so much with so little, and our churches do so little with so much.

Do not focus on what you cannot know. Focus on what you will receive. Focus on what you will do as a result. No more looking into the sky, yearning for the former things while wasting time on nonessential things. Let us surrender our will and agendas so the Holy Spirit can lead, empower, and manifest himself. And let us get back to doing what the New Testament calls and expects the body of Christ to do: to share the gospel, make disciples, and bring glory to God.

Read John 17:6-26. What differences do you see in this prayer of Jesus and the typical prayers we pray on Sunday mornings?

How much of your praying is directed toward you and your needs? How much is directed toward the lost, the mission of the church, worship, etc.?

Would you be willing to make a commitment to a weekly prayer group (that met at the church or in someone's home) for the purpose of increasing your reliance on prayer for your church? If no, why not?

Scripture memory verse for the week:

"But you will receive power when the Holy Spirit comes on you; and you will be my witnesses in Jerusalem, and in all Judea and Samaria, and to the ends of the earth." Acts 1:8

Prayer:

Holy Spirit, as I begin this journey through the book of Acts, I ask for your guidance and wisdom. I know there is much you desire to say to me and to my church. Open my heart and spirit to wait upon you. Open my eyes to see what you long to do in my church. Fill me with your power, Holy Trinity; with passion and commitment. I ask you to anoint all those who are on this devotional journey with me, that we may be united as one, that we may experience a new revelation of your presence, and that we may help your kingdom to come upon the earth. Amen.

Notes & reflections

Week Two:

<u>Good Trouble</u>

Read Acts 3 & 4

Have you ever said something that got you in trouble with your spouse or with a friend? Have you ever messed up an assignment at work and got in trouble with the manager or boss? Maybe you have gotten called into the principal's office at school? Yeah, we have all been in trouble before. We can't avoid trouble at times because we all make mistakes. It is just part of what it means to be human.

But have you ever *wanted* to get in trouble for something? Perhaps you felt that in order to draw attention to an issue or concern, the most significant way of accomplishing that was to intentionally get in trouble. Martin Luther King Jr., Vernon Johns, and other pioneers of the civil rights movement are excellent examples of wanting to get in trouble. Through their peaceful, nonviolent protests they were arrested, harassed, ridiculed, even killed—and in the process laid bare the bigotry of racism. They got into trouble.

Good trouble.

In this week's reading we find Peter and John likewise getting into good trouble. Chapter three presents the story of the miraculous healing of a beggar at the Beautiful Gate. Take time this week to re-read verses 1-10. Pay attention to the gestures, expressions, and actions that are described. Take special note of any words, phrases, or images that stand out in your mind.

Soon after this healing, the two disciples were cornered by a contingent of negative voices from the priests and Sadducees. This latter group didn't believe in the resurrection of the dead, so they were particularly perturbed that Peter and John were teaching *"...in Jesus the resurrection of the dead."* As a result, Peter and John were given a free night's stay in the Iron Bar Hotel.

"But many who heard the message believed; so the number of men who believed grew to about five thousand."

Wow! The church went from about 120 (Acts 1:15) to adding 3,000 (Acts 2:41) to now adding over 5,000! They were fast pushing the 10,000-member barrier! How did such incredible growth occur? Being a fisherman, Peter certainly had not received the sort of formal education that would produce a stunning orator of this caliber, capable of wooing the crowds to such levels of response. So how do we account for the massive influx of people responding to Peter's words? Simply put, as we saw last week: the power of the Holy Spirit. God was at work through the Holy Spirit, not only to empower Peter's words, but also to ready the hearts of those who were listening. Luke makes it plain in 4:8: *"Then Peter, **filled with the Holy Spirit**, said to them..."*

Not only does the Spirit empower the gospel to touch

the needs of listeners; he also empowers Christ-followers to speak with boldness and conviction. In just a few short verses (4:8-12) Peter lays it on them! Of course, the religious leaders were not happy about all that "Jesus talk." They were under the impression they had put an end to all of that rubbish a few weeks back. But here it was again, this time coming from a couple of scruffy fishermen with bad haircuts.

"When they saw the courage of Peter and John and realized that they were unschooled, ordinary men, they were astonished and they took note that these men had been with Jesus." Maybe you will want to take a little time and just dwell on that one sentence. It is powerful.

These men *had been with Jesus.*

The religious leaders could tell that, just as they could tell these were not a couple of fancy Greek scholars standing before them. Yet there was something compelling, different, and powerful about these two fishermen.

Would you say your church is compelling? Is there something different about your church that draws people to it? Is there obvious supernatural power in your church? If you can answer any of these questions with a "no," then perhaps we have not spent as much time with Jesus as we need to. Maybe we have not *been with Jesus* in such a way as to be compelling, different, and powerful.

Peter and John faced additional harassment at the hands of the religious establishment. Upon their release from prison, they went back and reported everything to the church. But pay attention to how the church responded to Peter and John's experience: *When they heard this, they raised their voices together in prayer to God.*

They prayed! We saw this last week, too. If you are start-ing to notice a pattern here in the early church, you are right. Treat yourself to some ice cream after your devotional time today!

So what exactly did the church pray for?

"Now, Lord, consider their threats and enable your servants to speak your word with great boldness. Stretch out your hand to heal and perform signs and wonders through the name of your holy servant Jesus." They prayed TO GET IN TROUBLE! They did not ask for God to keep them from harm. They did not ask for safety and security. They prayed for strength and courage, because they knew they were *not* going to be safe and secure! They did not lie low and wait for the heat to die down. They pleaded with God for even more miracles that would glorify Jesus.

They were asking to get into good trouble for honoring Jesus and serving God. They wanted the lost people around them to find hope and salvation in Jesus, and·they were will-ing to pay the price for it.

What are we willing to pay the price for? Are we willing to surrender something dear, comforting, or meaningful about our church if it will aid us in reaching the lost? Would we be bold or radical enough to pray like the early church did?

Be careful how you answer.

If you do not truly want the Holy Spirit's power, you had better not pray such a prayer, because look what happened: *"After they prayed, the place where they were meeting was shaken. And they were all filled with the Holy Spirit and spoke the word of God boldly."*

Uh-oh. They got exactly what they prayed for (and a little

shaking to go along with it!). They *spoke the word of God boldly.*
If we are serious about prayer, we are going to get in trouble.
If we are willing to return our churches to the New Testament
model, there are going to be many difficulties and obstacles.
There will be plenty of trouble to go around. The church in
Acts discovered this. We will too.

What might "good trouble" in your church look like?

**What are three things you could do to help make your
church compelling, different, and powerful?**

**So far, what are some of the critical elements in the life
of the early church?**

**In what ways do you need to "be with Jesus" more? In
what ways does your church need to be with Jesus?**

Scripture memory verse for the week:

*"Now, Lord, consider their threats and enable your
servants to speak your word with great boldness.
Stretch out your hand to heal and perform signs and
wonders through the name of your holy servant Jesus."*
Acts 4:29-30

Prayer:

Lord Jesus, I want to be more like Peter and John. I hunger for your power and presence to so fill my life that you may be glorified in all I say and do. I pray for my church to be more like the early church. Help me to be a prayer warrior who does not hesitate to call on your name for our ministries, our mission, and our heart for the lost. Together, may we as a church find more ways to use our resources to assist those in need. Send me to the people in my community who need the good news of Jesus Christ. Let me be a catalyst for leading our church into the world to minister and serve with great boldness, and with the assurance that you go before us to accomplish your divine will. Amen.

Notes & reflections

_____

_____

_____

_____

_____

_____

_____

_____

_____

_____

_____

_____

Week Three

Picking a Fight

Read Acts 5, 6 & 7

I am a great fan of the film *Braveheart*. Mel Gibson plays William Wallace, the 13th century Scot who was instrumental in fighting for, and helping to win, Scotland's independence from England. In fact, my maternal grandfather's ancestors once owned land in Scotland where William Wallace fought one of his battles.

There is a scene in the film where Wallace has assembled his motley troops on a hillside. Across the grassy plain are the far superior British troops. Wallace's men know they are out-numbered. The British troops have better weapons, archers, and cavalry. It is a foregone conclusion that the Scots will have to surrender and accept terms, which will drive them even deeper into debt slavery to England.

However, Wallace has other plans. He gives a stirring speech to his restive men about valor and freedom. When finished, he sees three representatives from the English army ride to the center of the plain. Before one of the Scottish lords can ride out to surrender to the English, Wallace spurs his horse forward. One of his generals asks, "Where are you going?"

Grinning, Wallace replies, "I'm going to pick a fight!"

And pick a fight he does! Instead of the soft, corrupt Scottish lords — whose lands and titles have been bestowed upon them by the English in exchange for their loyalty and support — the English officers come face-to-face with William Wallace. And he definitely is not interested in their terms. In fact, he has some terms of his own for the English.

In this week's reading we see two examples of people picking fights. The first is the tragic story of Ananias and Sapphira in Acts 5:1-11. This couple picked a fight with the Holy Spirit and lost.

Ananias and Sapphira sold a piece of land, just as Acts 4:34-35 describes. Yet this couple conspired together to keep some of the proceeds from the church: *"With his wife's full knowledge he kept back part of the money for himself."* The rest they presented to the apostles just as others had been doing. But the Holy Spirit can't be fooled. And because Peter was walking so closely in the Spirit, he immediately discerned that something was not right.

It was not that Ananias and Sapphira didn't have the right to keep the money from the sale of their own field. They certainly did. Peter even rhetorically points this out: *"Didn't it belong to you before it was sold? And after it was sold, wasn't the money at your disposal?"* The issue was not about the rights of the owner. It was about trying to deceive the church and the Holy Spirit.

Ananias and Sapphira wanted the church to believe the

amount they gave was the full amount of the sale. They wanted to impress people with their generosity. They wanted people to think highly of them for the generous sacrifice they were making. It was all about the image, the acclaim, and the prestige they could have in front of others. Peter told Ananias, *"You have not lied just to human beings but to God."* In other words, it was one thing to lie to the apostles. But the couple tried to slip one past God by pretending they had given the full amount, when in reality they had deliberately held back.

In essence, they tried to pick a fight with the Holy Spirit, and the two paid for this folly with their lives. We may be curious about why the outcome was so much more devastating than the deception itself. It is a powerful and sobering reminder that shows us God is very, very concerned about unity and truth within the church.

The second instance also happens in chapter five: *"Then the high priest and all his associates, who were members of the party of the Sadducees, were filled with jealousy"* (v. 17). The religious establishment grew increasingly bitter about what the early church was doing. Just as we saw in chapter four, they arrested the apostles and hauled them before the Sanhedrin. They interrogated them. *"We gave you strict orders not to teach in this name,"* he said. *"Yet you have filled Jerusalem with your teaching and are determined to make us guilty of this man's blood."* And once again Peter responded boldly (remember what the church prayed for in 4:29?). The apostles and the early church were obligated to follow the commands of God over the selfish, corrupt, and controlling religious elite. Needless to say, that did not sit well…again! *"When they heard this, they were furious and wanted to put them to death."*

However, there was a member of the Sanhedrin—Gamaliel—who obviously was a bit wiser and more thoughtful than the rest. He told the elders and leaders that there had been other so-called messiahs, Theudas and Judas the Galilean in particular. They had followers. They had rhetoric and slogans. They had popular support. Both thought they were the long-awaited answer Israel needed. And yet *"[Theudas] was killed, all his followers were dispersed, and it all came to nothing."* *"[Judas the Galilean] too was killed, and all his followers were scattered."* Obviously, the popular revolutions kept falling short.

Gamaliel then told his colleagues something vital: *"Leave these men alone! Let them go! For if their purpose or activity is of human origin, it will fail. But if it is from God, you will not be able to stop these men;* **you will only find yourselves fighting against God.**"

The Sanhedrin, fearful of losing power and status, had picked a fight with the early church. And as Gamaliel said, if this was something merely of human origin and power, it would eventually collapse, just as the previous uprisings had. But on the other hand, if this "Jesus thing" really *WAS* of God, then the Sanhedrin had just picked a fight with the Almighty himself!

As we seek God's guidance to help churches reclaim the New Testament model, we will encounter those who oppose such actions. They may be from other churches or denominations. They may be from people or groups within our own churches. They may even be from within our own families. Jesus made plain the cost of following him in Matthew 10.

People will say we are being "unrealistic." We will be told that we are ruining the church and driving good members away. There will be accusations that our ideas and actions are crippling the church's budget, or that we are alienating people. You may even be accused of being brainwashed! Some of my friends who have supported church transformation have been accused of being weak-minded and easily swayed by my ideas. You can be sure that if you want to see the church regain its power and influence, there will be those who are more than willing to pick a fight.

If the dream we pursue and the vision we strive for is indeed of human origin, or attempted in our own limited power, then it will most certainly fail. However, if we are truly seeking the guidance and wisdom of the Holy Spirit — if we are seeking to please God above people in all things — if we are grounded in the Word and in prayer — *if what we are doing IS OF GOD*...then someone will be picking a fight with God. They will be trying to tear down or discredit the work of the Lord himself. NOT a place you'd want to be!

In one church I encountered a group of controllers and bullies who refused to see what God wanted to do in their church. They had always enjoyed their entitlements, comforts, and influence. Because they were not getting their own selfish way, they actively campaigned to get people to stop coming to worship. They wanted to see the turnaround fail. They did not care about the health, growth, or future of their church (and some of these were lifelong members). All they wanted was to remain in control.

They thought what was happening was just some flaky idea of the pastor and some leaders who the pastor had brainwashed. But in reality it was a movement of the Holy Spirit, and these bitter people found themselves fighting against

God. As the church moved forward — despite the protests, negativity, and persecution — *every one of the people who were fighting against God were removed*. Most stopped attending. A few transferred to other churches in the area. All of them were exposed; God defeated all their poisonous work. They had picked a fight with the Lord and they came out on the losing end. Once they left, the church immediately become healthier, stronger, more missional, and more worshipful.

As you continue to read Acts, attend worship, pray, and serve others, ask the Holy Spirit to help you see what his plan and purpose is for your church. Pray for your pastor and church leaders who are diligently seeking to map out where God is leading your congregation. Remember our central verse: *"But you will receive power when the Holy Spirit comes on you; and you will be my witnesses in Jerusalem, and in all Judea and Samaria, and to the ends of the earth"* (Acts 1:8). The goal for your church is to become the living embodiment of this verse. You want to be so filled with the Holy Spirit that you are totally consumed with revealing the glory of Jesus Christ everywhere. Everyone should be welcomed and invited to join in this journey. And if it is of mere human design and strength, you will know very quickly. But if it's *truly from God…*

What was your reaction to the story of Ananias and Sapphira?

How do we try and deceive God in the church today? What do we "hold back" from him, while still claiming to have given our all?

What does the story of Ananias and Sapphira tell us about how God views deception in the church? Why do you think this is such a serious thing?

Are you interested in pursuing the biblical mission of the church? Are you "fighting against God" because you can't have your own way or your own comforts? What would God say to you if this were the case?

What if your church began to pursue a new future that involved small group gatherings, prayer gatherings and prayer teams, short-term mission trips, outreach to the poor and needy, and a firm dedication to making Christ known both near and far?

What would excite you about this? What would frighten you?

What would you be most afraid of losing or having to surrender in order to accomplish these things?

What are you willing to do in order to make these things happen for the glory of Jesus Christ?

Scripture memory verse for the week:

"For if their purpose or activity is of human origin, it will fail. But if it is from God, you will not be able to stop these men; you will only find yourselves fighting against God." Acts 5:38-39

 ## Prayer:

Holy Spirit, help me to fight against the spiritual powers of evil that want to destroy your church. Give me the strength to pray without ceasing for the mission and purpose of our church, that Christ may truly be known and glorified. I do not want to fight against you. I want to willingly be part of what you are doing in the church. I pray for my pastor and our church leaders, that you will supernaturally bless them with your vision, perseverance, and power to lead us in your steps. May you be glorified and lifted up in my life this day, Lord Jesus; and may you transform the innermost parts of me so that I fully conform to your image. In the name of the Father, and of the Son, and of the Holy Spirit. Amen.

Notes & reflections

_____

_____

_____

_____

_____

_____

_____

_____

_____

_____

Week Four:

Obstacles and Opportunities

Read Acts 8 & 9

What happens when the church of Jesus Christ forgets its mission and reason for existence? What happens when the church puts more focus and resources on those inside the building than on those outside? What happens when fulfilling the mission of Jesus Christ takes second, third, or even fourth place to keeping members happy? One consequence is that those members begin to mistakenly assume the church leaders exist to serve them. We see the beginnings of this in Acts 6:1-4.

An issue arose over the distribution of food between the Greek-speaking and the Hebrew-speaking Jews. We are told the Twelve got together and decided, *"It would not be right for us to neglect the ministry of the word of God in order to wait on tables"* (6:2). They did not say this because they were unconcerned about the hungry or the widows. Far from it! But from their statement *"it would not be right,"* we can glean that some in the early church wanted, or expected, the Twelve to cater to them and wait on them. It would seem someone had already suggested that the Twelve needed to spend more time visiting and handing out food, instead of all that praying and teaching. One of the most obvious indicators that a church has turned inward and become selfish is when leaders are expected to cater to the whims and personal preferences of the members.

Another thing that happens is the church loses its vision for mission and reaching the lost. Following the tragic martyrdom of Stephen we read, *"on that day a great persecution broke out against the church in Jerusalem, and all except the apostles were scattered throughout Judea and Samaria"* (8:1). As we have seen, the church at Jerusalem had been growing by leaps and bounds. Their numbers were increasingly dramatically. And in the midst of all this good growth they began to lose sight of their mission and purpose. Jesus had told them in 1:8, *"But you will receive power when the Holy Spirit comes on you; and you will be my witnesses in Jerusalem, and in all Judea and Samaria, and to the ends of the earth."* But yet by chapter eight they were still in Jerusalem.

Notice where people went on the day the persecution broke out against the church: throughout *Judea* and *Samaria*. The very places Jesus said they would be his witnesses. But because Jerusalem represented a comfort zone, a safe and predictable place for the church, they had largely given up on the idea of going anywhere else. The Jerusalem church had become content to add to its numbers, but was not fulfilling the mission of Jesus Christ. I do not think it is a coincidence that persecution comes against the Jerusalem church at this point. It seems to be God's way of forcing them to move outside their comfort and security, and to engage the world with the good news.

In what ways do you think your church might be like the Jerusalem church?

Why do our comfort zones and personal preferences so quickly take precedence over the commands of Christ?

How do you think the people felt about having to leave "their church" and go into Judea and Samaria?

But look what Philip, Peter, and John accomplished for the kingdom once they stopped playing it safe in Jerusalem and re-focused on the mission of Jesus (see 8:4-40). The persecution and obstacles the church faced actually became opportunities for the spread of the gospel.

Few of us really enjoy change. As creatures of habit, we prefer our routines and we fight for the preservation of our comforts. But what we always overlook in the midst of dealing with change are the opportunities God has in store for us. Take Saul for example.

Chapter nine tells the well-known story of Saul's dramatic conversion experience. Here was a vengeful, bitter man who was determined to stamp out this growing sect of Jesus followers. He had the influence and authority of the chief priest on his side. He had arrest warrants for anyone who was

found worshiping Jesus. Saul was one of the most passion-
ate anti-Jesus people around. But notice that while the church
was suffering because of Saul, God was orchestrating an even
greater opportunity for the church.

*"But the Lord said to Ananias, 'Go! This man is my chosen
instrument* **to proclaim my name to the Gentiles and their
kings** *and to the people of Israel. I will show him how much he must
suffer for my name'"* (9:15-16). The one doing the persecuting of
the church would become the greatest defender of the church,
and one of the greatest theological minds Christianity has ever
produced. It was a move from obstacle to opportunity. And
notice that even within the call upon Saul's life, God made
it clear that there would be more persecution and obstacles
ahead. But that just meant more opportunities, as we shall
discover as we move deeper into Acts.

Check out Acts 9:23: *"After many days had gone by, there was
a conspiracy among the Jews to kill [Saul]..."*

And 9:29: *"He talked and debated with the Hellenistic Jews, but
they tried to kill him."*

We even see that when Saul visited Jerusalem for the first
time following his conversion, he needed the support and
confirmation of Barnabas before the church would accept him.
In each of these times of persecution, in each of the obstacles
Saul faced, God opened up doors of opportunity for the message of Jesus to be heard and received. How do we know this?
*"Then the church throughout Judea, Galilee and Samaria enjoyed a
time of peace and was strengthened. Living in the fear of the Lord
and encouraged by the Holy Spirit, it increased in numbers."*

Obstacles lead to opportunities; persecution leads to pos-
sibilities — if we are willing to trust the guiding hand of God

and the call of Jesus Christ. The church does not exist to cater to you or me, to serve up the kind of music we enjoy, or to keep us comfortable and content. The church exists to spread the good news of the kingdom across the world so that Christ may be glorified. Anything less is not a true biblical expression of the church.

Where do you see obstacles or persecution in your church?

Describe a time where an obstacle you encountered led to an opportunity.

What is the pastor's role in the church (hint: see Ephesians 4:11-13)? What is the role of each church member?

Scripture memory verse for the week:

"Therefore, go and make disciples of all the nations, baptizing them in the name of the Father and the Son and the Holy Spirit. Teach these new disciples to obey all the commands I have given you. And be sure of this: I am with you always, even to the end of the age." Matthew 28:19-20

Prayer:

Lord Jesus, I want to be part of the unleashing of the Holy Spirit in my church. I understand that in order to follow you fully, and to love you with all my heart, soul, mind, and strength, I will be persecuted. People will say negative things about me. Lord, you endured the scorn and abuse of those you came to save. You said that if they persecuted you, they would persecute your followers as well. Grant me the courage and perseverance to stand strong in the face of opposition, so that my witness may be glorifying to your holy name. I also ask that you help me to know my spiritual giftedness for ministry. Your Word declares that you have given me gifts to be used for the building up on the body of Christ. Stir up your gifts in me, that I am joyfully and faithfully fulfill my role and calling in my church. Amen.

Notes & reflections

Week Five:

<u>Surely Not, Lord!</u>

Read Acts 10 & 11

Simon Peter and the original disciples of Jesus are often accused of not "getting it" much of the time. Despite the continued statements about Jesus' death and resurrection, the Twelve never quite understood things, at least not until after Jesus rose from the dead. Then, as we have seen so far in Acts, these men became exceptionally bold and confident through the Holy Spirit. But Peter did have a bit of a relapse.

God was up to something so unbelievable, so inconceivable and outrageous, it took Peter a few tries to get it all down. In chapter 10 we read about a vision God sent to Peter. In it God shows Peter a big picnic blanket covered with all sorts of critters, and his instructions to Peter are to *"Kill and eat"* (10:13). This posed a major problem for Peter, as some of the animals in the vision were considered unclean according to the Law of Moses. So he responded as any good Jewish boy should: *"Surely not, Lord! I have never eaten anything impure or unclean"* (10:14).

Surely not, Lord!

This sounds like the reply we often have to something unexpected (or unwanted) that God seeks to do in, with, or through us. We think everything should happen just as it did in the past. We like the predictability and the assurance that we have certain things all figured out. No surprises for us in our spiritual journeys, thank you very much!

God responded to Peter. *"Do not call anything impure that God has made clean"* (10:15). Uh-oh! This was something new and different. This was not the reply Peter was expecting. He was waiting for the heavenly voice to say something like, "Good job, Peter. You remembered your lessons in Old Testament law!" And so we catch a glimpse of the old Peter—the pre-Holy Spirit Peter—when we are told, *this happened three times* (10:16). It took God three tries to get the message into Peter's mind and heart. And in 10:23-24, we see it takes another full day of wrestling and pondering before Peter can come to grips with the fact that God was not doing things the way he had before.

Peter needed to be prepared for an encounter with a God-fearing Gentile named Cornelius. Now we know Jews and Samaritans did not mix. Jews considered Samaritans "half-breeds" and looked down on them. Being around Samaritans would not make a Jew unclean. However, a Gentile most definitely would. And there was Peter, traipsing along to Caesarea, getting ready for the second biggest shock of his life.

God had long been at work in Cornelius and his household. He had been preparing this Roman soldier for entry into the kingdom of heaven. We should never forget that God has been at work in the lives of people around us long before we encounter them. It is not our job to convince or convict. That is the work of the Holy Spirit. Ours is only to do the task for which God has brought a person into our sphere of influence. As Peter preached, the Holy Spirit fell upon Cornelius, his household, and his closest friends. It is a relief to know that the outcome is up to God and not us.

But wait a minute...

The Holy Spirit...being received by...*Gentiles?*

Surely not, Lord!

Yet that is exactly what happened. Peter had received a vision indicating that all animals were clean to eat *in readiness for something of even greater significance:* that every person, Gentile as well as Jew, could receive the Holy Spirit. The fledgling Christian sect was not just for Greek-speaking or Hebrew-speaking Jews. The movement of Jesus Christ into the world had now reached across one of the oldest social, cultural, and religious barriers. Gentile Christians were now on the same level ground as the Jewish Christians. God had done something unbelievable, inconceivable, and outrageous. Surely not, Lord!

We may not say those exact words, but in our hearts we sometimes think them. If we get the sense that God is trying to do something we have not seen before, we declare "Surely not, Lord!" We think God would never want us to change our worship service in order to better reach the lost, or to use our spacious buildings to shelter the homeless. We cannot imagine that God would want us to devote more of our financial resources to missions, outreach, and taking the gospel into the world. Too many churches, for far too long, have managed and controlled things so tightly that the Holy Spirit can't get a word in edgewise. And when he does catch a break and see an opening, we throw our hands up and say "Surely not, Lord!"

It is funny: for a long time the church said "Surely not, Lord!" when it came to African Americans and the abolition of slavery. For a long time the church said "Surely not, Lord!" when it came to women clergy. Today we still exclaim "Surely not, Lord!" when it comes to the immigrant, the homeless, the Democrat, the Republican, the homosexual, the poor, the uninsured. Perhaps if we spent more time on our faces in prayer, seeking the will and presence of Almighty God, and less time lining up the things we think God should not do, Christianity might be able to reclaim much of its spiritual power and effectiveness. To reclaim our New Testament roots, we must be willing to allow God to do new things in our churches.

Pay attention to what happened in the Jerusalem church when word got back to them that Peter has been hanging out with a Gentile: *"The apostles and the believers throughout Judea heard that the Gentiles also had received the word of God. So when Peter went up to Jerusalem, the circumcised believers criticized him and said, 'You went into the house of uncircumcised men and ate with them'"* (11:1-3). Yes, you guessed it. "The Gentiles know Jesus and have the Holy Spirit? Surely not, Lord!" Or as the infamous "Seven Last Words of the Church" state: "We've never done it that way before!"

In the Old Testament, the prophet Isaiah declared:

"This is what the LORD says — he who made a way through the sea, a path through the mighty waters, who drew out the chariots and

horses, the army and reinforcements together, and they lay there,
never to rise again, extinguished, snuffed out like a wick: 'Forget the
former things; do not dwell on the past. See, I am doing a new thing!
Now it springs up; do you not perceive it?'" (43:16-19)

Isaiah had to deal with the same attitude from the people
of his day. The Israelites had come to believe that the *only*
way God could work was like he did in the Exodus, when
he delivered his captive people from Pharaoh's grasp. Notice
how Isaiah refers to the path through the sea, and the chariots
and horses of Egypt that perished. It was as if he was saying,
"Yes, that's how God did it in the past. But just wait...!" He
continues by telling them to *forget* the former things! Let go
of the assumption that God can only act in one specific way.
"See, I am doing a new thing!"

That 'new thing,' of course, would be Jesus Christ. And as
we know, the religious leaders and those in power failed to
recognize that God was not limited to acting only as he had
in the past. As has been said, God's plans are eternal but his
methods are always changing.

Without the inclusion of the Gentiles into the plan of
salvation — without Peter's acceptance of God's vision and
the knowledge that the Holy One was up to something *very*
different — we would not be Christian today (unless we were
Jews who had confessed Jesus as Messiah). We would still
be lost in our sins, fears, and brokenness. If that age-old barrier of separation had not come down through Cornelius and
Peter, the history of the world would look a lot different.

"Surely not, Lord!"??

Let us be careful when we are tempted to say that because

the next great advancement of God's kingdom may be await-
ing the very thing we don't think he will do. Thank God that
Peter finally got it. Thank God that the Holy Spirit has been
made available to all who surrender their lives to the lordship
of Jesus Christ. As the apostle Paul would later go on to write:
*"in this new life, it doesn't matter if you are a Jew or a Gentile,
circumcised or uncircumcised, barbaric, uncivilized, slave, or free.
Christ is all that matters, and he lives in all of us"* (Colossians
3:11).

**Can you think of instances in your life or the life of the
church when "Surely not, Lord!" was the central response?**

**Perhaps Peter was being a little thick and didn't quite
grasp the significance of God's vision to him. What other
reason(s) might there be for God telling Peter the same
thing three times?**

**Read Mark 7:14-19. What does Jesus say here that fore-
shadows the vision God gives to Peter?**

**The church at Antioch will go on to play a key role in the
mission of Jesus Christ. According to Acts 11:19-21, who is
the gospel reaching by this time?**

How long do Saul and Barnabas stay in Antioch? What

were they doing during this time? Why is this important in the life of the church?

Whom do you know in your church who can assume this kind of teaching and leadership role?

What feelings are you having at this point in your journey through Acts? What is the Holy Spirit saying to you about your church? What actions do you feel the Holy Spirit is calling you to, personally?

 Scripture memory verse for the week:

"And no one puts new wine into old wineskins. For the wine would burst the wineskins, and the wine and the skins would both be lost. New wine calls for new wineskins." Mark 2:22

 Prayer:

Lord Jesus, there have been times when my response to you was "Surely not, Lord!" I didn't understand – or didn't want to understand – what you were asking of me. I preferred the false safety and empty promises of my own selfishness. But now, dear Christ, I offer myself to you fully and obediently. Please use me to help bring about a new thing in my life and in my church. Continue to teach me your Word. Continue to reveal my sinfulness. Continue to help me walk in your holiness. And may my personal preferences and agendas never become so

rigid that I cannot lay them aside when you call me to. In the name of the Father, the Son, and the Holy Spirit. Amen.

Notes & reflections

_____

_____

_____

_____

_____

_____

_____

_____

_____

_____

_____

_____

_____

_____

_____

_____

_____

_____

_____

_____

_____

_____

_____

_____

_____

Week Six:

Endings and Beginnings

Read Acts 12 & 13

Chapters twelve and thirteen represent a significant turning point in Acts. It is an ending and a beginning. It is good-bye and hello.

Chapter twelve details another arrest and imprisonment for Peter in Jerusalem. His rap sheet was beginning to look like Jackie Chan's emergency room chart! However, it was not the religious leaders behind it this time. Instead it was King Herod Agrippa, who just happened to be a grandson of Herod the Great—the same man who tried to have the infant Jesus killed (see Matthew 2). When Herod Agrippa had James, the brother of John, martyred, the king gained additional favor with the Jewish people. The spread of Christianity in and around Jerusalem continued to meet with resistance and contention from the Jews.

So Herod thought to himself, "Hey, if I got such a great response from doing away with James, I could really score some serious points if I also did away with that pesky fisherman, Peter."

Now pay attention. Luke tells us *"when [King Herod] saw that this met with approval among the Jews, he proceeded to seize Peter also."* **This happened during the Festival of Unleavened Bread** (12:3). There is an obvious parallel between what happened to Peter and what happened to Jesus.

Jesus was arrested and tried in the hours of his passion, which definitely pleased the religious leaders, who had persuaded the people this was a good thing. It happened to Jesus during the Passover as well. So we have an interesting parallel between these events with Peter, and the events that Peter had witnessed in the final hours of Jesus' life.

Also, take notice of the response of the church: *So Peter was kept in prison, but the church was **earnestly praying** to God for him* (12:5). The Greek word translated 'earnestly' is *ektenós*. It means strenuously or fervently. It can also mean *extended or stretched out, to its necessary or full potential*, and *without undue let up*. In other words, the church was praying for Peter constantly. Without stopping. Going beyond what was asked or needed. They put their own needs and selves aside in order to intercede for Peter.

What would it take for you and your church to learn to pray *ektenos* — with determination, commitment, and passion?

Why do you think we spend so little time in prayer?

If your church prayed together the way the church in Acts did, what sort of results do you think you might see?

Following his supernatural escape, Peter reported back to the church how "...*the Lord had brought him out of prison. 'Tell James and the other brothers and sisters about this,' he said, and then he left for another place.*" Obviously, Peter knew he needed to lay low for a while. Plus, he did not want to bring any further persecution against the church by his presence. So he disappears, almost literally.

Except for a brief appearance in Acts 15:7-11 at the Jerusalem Council, this is the final appearance of Peter in the book of Acts. He drops out of the story altogether. Other than a reference in Galatians (2:11-14) and quite possibly some time spent in Corinth (1 Corinthians 3:22), we do not have much else on Peter, beyond the two New Testament letters that bear his name. Historically, it is believed that Peter ended up in Rome and was martyred by Emperor Nero, most likely around 64-66 CE. So we say goodbye to Peter in the chronicles of the early church...but we say hello to a new beginning in chapter thirteen.

The focus shifts now to Barnabas and Saul. "*While they were worshiping the Lord and fasting, the Holy Spirit said, 'Set apart for me Barnabas and Saul for the work to which I have called them.' So after they had fasted and prayed, they placed their hands on them and sent them off*" (13:2-3). Within these two verses we see once again the reliance upon the Holy Spirit, the ongoing immediacy of prayer, as well as a strong connection between worship and fasting. These are all clues to realizing how we can transition today's church toward a more biblical foundation.

A young man named John Mark joined Barnabas and Saul (13:5) on what is commonly known as the first missionary journey. In 13:9, we find the first mention of Saul's name change to Paul, indicating the death of his old self and the *new creation* (2 Corinthians 5:17) he had become in Christ Jesus.

It is interesting to note how Paul's preaching in Pisidian Antioch (Acts 13:13-41) mirrored the sermon of Peter at Pentecost (Acts 2:14-40), as well as Stephen's message to the Sanhedrin (Acts 7:2-53). Paul's custom was to visit the local synagogues in whatever city he was in and present the good news of Jesus Christ there. But he soon discovered that many Jews were unwilling to listen. *"When the Jews saw the crowds, they were filled with jealousy. They began to contradict what Paul was saying and heaped abuse on him. Then Paul and Barnabas answered them boldly: 'We had to speak the word of God to you first. Since you reject it and do not consider yourselves worthy of eternal life, we now turn to the Gentiles'"* (13:45-46).

We have already seen how God led Peter to bridge the Jew-Gentile divide in the home of Cornelius. The church discovered that the Holy Spirit was indeed intended for all who claimed faith in Jesus. Now Paul and Barnabas were commissioned as missionaries to actively take the gospel into the Gentile world. And look at the outcome: *"When the Gentiles heard this, they were glad and honored the word of the Lord.... The word of the Lord spread through the whole region"* (13:48-49).

If we are wondering why the focus of Acts shifts from the Jerusalem church to the missionary church planting efforts of Paul, Barnabas, Silas, and others, let us revisit the original command of Jesus: *"...you will be my witnesses in Jerusalem, and* *in all Judea and Samaria, **and to the ends of the earth**"* (1:8). We saw in chapter six how the Jerusalem church had already started to turn inward. Subtly, they began to focus more on themselves — their comforts and entitlements — than on carrying out the Acts 1:8 commission. We saw God use an outbreak of persecution to "motivate" them to get up and get going.

The purpose of the church is to bring glory to God through Jesus Christ. It is to share the good news of God's reconciliation with all people, and to reveal an alternative community — God's kingdom — here on earth. The story of the early church is like ripples spreading across water. The movement began in Jerusalem but could not be contained there. It went into Judea and Samaria, but that was not the end because Christ calls his people into *the entire world* with his message of new life and discipleship (Matthew 28:19-20).

Many churches today rarely ever fulfill the mission and purpose of the church in their own Jerusalems. Fewer reach into their Judeas. Even less go to Samaria. And only a small percentage takes seriously the call to go to the ends of the earth. This helps to explain why so many people across the world have never heard the name of Jesus Christ, despite the advances in technology, communication, and transportation. We have not gone to the ends of the earth as we have been instructed. We have erroneously assumed that sort of thing is for professional missionaries. "We'll give them a few dollars a year in support," churches rationalize, "but we're not going *over there*." No, we would rather be like the Jerusalem church and hunker down behind our walls and assume Christ's commands are for someone else. We must renew our commitment to take seriously this missional mandate.

Let us keep in mind what we are seeing repeatedly in Acts: whenever Christians step out in faith and in the power of the Holy Spirit, whenever Christians are firmly grounded and bathed in prayer, the gospel advances. People are saved. The church grows. Disciples are made. *"And the disciples were filled with joy and with the Holy Spirit."*

Would you like for people to say of your church, "They're always filled with joy and with the Holy Spirit!"? What a marvelous testimony! We can have that, if we are willing to pray, to let the Holy Spirit shape our lives, and to be obedient to the command and commission of Christ. In doing so, we may see the end of some things and the bold new beginning of others!

Do you have any thoughts or ideas on why Peter suddenly drops out of the Acts narrative and the focus shifts to Paul and Barnabas?

How would you feel about the possibility of participating in a short-term mission trip overseas? What fears do you have?

What fears do you have about being a missionary to the people in your "Jerusalem" or "Samaria"?

Picture God saying one thing to your church at this moment. What would it be?

What is one thing that has ended for you in relation to the church? What is one thing that has begun?

Scripture memory verse for the week:

One day as these men were worshiping the Lord and fasting, the Holy Spirit said, "Dedicate Barnabas and Saul for the special work to which I have called them." So after more fasting and prayer, the men laid their hands on them and sent them on their way.   Acts 13:2-3

Prayer:

Holy Spirit, you are leading your church back to its roots in the New Testament. What I see in Acts is what you desire for your church to be and do. There are times when the things you ask of me seem too great or unbearable. I foolishly think I have to do it all on my own and in my own strength. But I remember that you are always with me. You have equipped me for every task. You have gifted me for ministry. Put an end to the things in me that are unholy and not of you. And begin now to show me how and where I am to minister and serve, so that our church may grow like the early church did. In the blessed and sacred name of Jesus. Amen.

Notes & reflections

Week Seven:

<u>Ministry is Messy!</u>

Read Acts 14, 15, & 16

Christians like to keep things neat and orderly. We prefer to have a place for everything and everything in its place. Even the name of my tribe, 'United METHODist,' indicates we have structured, methodical ways of doing and being. There is nothing wrong with this. All human structures and systems need some form of order and process. However, keeping things all sparkly and pristine does not mesh with the radical call to make disciples, because making disciples means entering into peoples' lives.

Dr. Lawson Stone, one of my Old Testament professors in seminary, said, "You cannot love someone without being interested in learning how that person came to be who they are." And in order to learn those things, we have to accept that our orderly little Christian world will get dirty, broken, and out-of-place. Nobody's life is squeaky clean and perfectly ordered. In the church we like to pretend that is the way our lives are. We wear the appropriate "mask" when we are with other church folk so they will not discover the truth about us. We convince ourselves that we have it all together, so much so that we actively avoid getting to know non-Christians. We do not engage in authentic ministry to the lost—the hurting, the needy, the hungry, the homeless, the mentally challenged, the foreigner, or the abused—because deep down we know it will cost us something. It will not be smooth, convenient, or tidy. It cannot be contained in a little box we can open and close whenever it suits us. Ministry is messy.

You would not have to tell that to Barnabas and Paul. In our readings for this week we see several examples of how messy it is to share the gospel, to enter into peoples' lives, and to allow God to use us. Beginning in chapter fourteen we find the two missionaries in Lystra. Paul healed a lame man and the citizens mistakenly assumed he and Barnabas were avatars of the Greek gods. They were ready to offer up sacrifices in honor of Paul and Barnabas. Paul pleaded with them, trying to get them to understand it was the work of the living God who purposed the miracle. *"Even with these words, they had difficulty keeping the crowd from sacrificing to them"* (14:18).

But things were about to get messier still. *"Then some Jews came from Antioch and Iconium and won the crowd over. They stoned Paul and dragged him outside the city, thinking he was dead"* (14:19). OUCH! There's nothing orderly or efficient about all of this. It is chaos, pure and simple. In seeking to help a handicapped man, things got messy.

Or consider the turmoil of the Jerusalem Council in chapter fifteen. Often called "the first church board meeting," there was not much quiet and meticulous there. A serious issue had arisen in the young church. *"Certain people came down from*

Judea to Antioch and were teaching the believers: 'Unless you are circumcised, according to the custom taught by Moses, you cannot be saved.' This brought Paul and Barnabas into sharp dispute and debate with them" (15:1-2).

Some Jewish Christians were operating under the assumption that circumcision, according the Law of Moses, was needed *in addition* to the grace of Jesus Christ. They wanted all the new Gentile Christians to be circumcised like they were, so they would fit into the Jewish system of thinking and behaving. Some of the church leaders had a major problem with this, so they convened a council to deliberate the issue and seek resolution.

The root issue here was the identity of Christians and the church. Up to this point, Christianity was seen as just a minor Jewish sect, a variation on traditional teachings, a fringe element. For the most part, the church still looked, talked, and acted in very Jewish ways. But now there were Gentiles to contend with. How did they fit into what (at the time) was a predominately Jewish movement? Did they need to become like the Jews who had received Christ? Some said yes. Others, emphatically no. If you have ever been in a church business meeting with a hotly contested issue, you have some idea of how this might have played out! *This brought Paul and Barnabas into **sharp dispute** and debate with them.*

Peter, in his final appearance in Acts, reminded the council of his encounter with Cornelius, and firmly stated, *"Now then, why do you try to test God by putting on the necks of Gentiles a yoke that neither we nor our ancestors have been able to bear? No! We believe it is through the grace of our Lord Jesus that we are saved, just as they are"* (15:10-11). He wisely recognized that the Jews had never been able to keep the Law of Moses, so why expect or assume the Gentiles could? Besides, it was not adherence to the law that brought salvation, but only grace through faith. Then James, the brother of the Lord and the acknowledged leader of the Jerusalem church, addressed the council: *"It is my judgment, therefore, that we should not make it difficult for the Gentiles who are turning to God. Instead we should write to them, telling them to abstain from food polluted by idols, from sexual immorality, from the meat of strangled animals and from blood"* (15:19-20). The issue of identity had been resolved. From that point on, Christianity would follow a different path from that of Judaism.

But the church today still struggles with sticky, uncomfortable issues that require discernment and wisdom. Despite our best efforts to keep things tidy, the sins and problems of human lives infiltrates our churches. We regularly face questions such as how should the church minister to sex offenders in their community, or who want to attend their worship services? How should a divorced couple—who both desire to attend the same church—be integrated into its life and practices? How should unsupervised children or youth in the neighborhood be ministered to? All these, and many others, cause us to stop and evaluate our spiritual identity. Who are we as a church? What do we stand for? Which commands of Christ have we chosen to obey and which ones have we chosen to ignore? Which individual or people group receives our attention or ministry, and which ones do not?

Ministry is messy.

Finally, look at the mess Paul and Barnabas got into in chapter 16. Paul landed both of them in hot water when he exorcised a demonic spirit from a slave girl (16:16-18): *"When her owners realized that their hope of making money was gone, they seized Paul and Silas and dragged them into the marketplace to face the authorities"* (16:19). Things got messier, and more painful, after that: *"The crowd joined in the attack against Paul and Silas, and the magistrates ordered them to be stripped and beaten with rods. After they had been severely flogged, they were thrown into prison"* (16:21-22). What should have been a time of rejoicing — the freeing of the girl from demonic possession — actually stirred up rage and opposition among the masses.

Even the encounter with the jailer (16:25-34) was chaotic. There was an earthquake, the prison fell apart around their ears, doors and chains broke open, and to top it off, the guard tried to commit suicide! This certainly was not your typical response to a Sunday morning altar call. The jailer took Paul and Barnabas home, cleaned them up, and accepted the salvation offered in Jesus Christ (I've always wondered what happened to the other prisoners the jailer was supposed to be guarding...?). There wasn't anything orthodox or well ordered or safe about that situation. It was a gigantic mess — but one in which God was still sovereign and used everything to draw others to Jesus Christ.

If we are serious about becoming a church like the one we see in Acts, we need to prepare ourselves for messiness. Ministry means getting into relationships with people who need help and who need Jesus. It means befriending them, assisting them, and loving them, even when it is painful or inconvenient for us to do so. God did not choose to leave us in our sin and desperation. He became like us, something that was painful (and quite likely inconvenient) so we would not remain slaves to sin and death. Paul, writing in Philippians 2:6-8 tells us, "*[Jesus], being in very nature God, did not consider equality with God something to be used to his own advantage; rather, he made himself nothing by taking the very nature of a servant, being made in human likeness. And being found in appearance as a man, he humbled himself by becoming obedient to death — even death on a cross!*" The church of Jesus Christ must do the same. We must allow ourselves to get messy, to get dirty, in order that we may present and represent Christ.

Jesus became like us. He willingly entered into the darkness, foulness, and brokenness of our human existence in order to redeem us and set us free. In fact, Jesus became our sin (2 Corinthians 5:21) on the cross. The purpose of the incarnation was to meet us where we are and deliver us into a far better place. It is the mission and purpose of the church to continue that incarnation. We are to go (remember Acts 1:8) where the need and hurt is, and to be "*the salt of the earth...*" and "*...the light of the world*" (Matthew 5:13-14). We are to be and do for others what Christ himself was and did for us.

This is one place where the church today has all but lost its New Testament identity. Most churches continue to operate in what is called an "attractional mode." The premise is that we need to draw — attract — people to our church buildings. Once there, we can minister to their needs and share Jesus with them. Almost all evangelistic outreach efforts still operate under this concept, despite the fact that twenty-first century people have little-to-no interest in going to church buildings. This approach worked well in the days of Christendom, but no longer.

If we are to recapture the original model of church, then

we must leave behind our padded pews and stained glass windows and go where the needs are. We must be willing to meet people on their own "turf." Today there are Bible studies and worship services meeting in tattoo shops, bars, and a myriad of other places "outside" the boundaries of the traditional church. We can no longer afford to sit in our gilded sanctuaries, wistfully yearning for the old days when everybody came to church. Christians must grab hold of Jesus Christ and allow him to take them out of their comfort zones and into the darkness, where light shines brightest and best.

Anything less and we are not the church.

Messy? Most definitely!

Just ask Paul and Barnabas. Just ask Jesus.

In what ways have you seen or experienced Christians or churches wanting everything to remain neat and orderly?

What aspect of the idea "ministry is messy" is most troubling or difficult for you?

Have you had an experience where you helped or ministered to someone and things got messy? How did you encounter Jesus in that experience?

How can individuals and churches serve others in a Christ-like way, yet maintain proper boundaries for safety and accountability?

Do you know anyone whose life is a mess, who needs Jesus Christ? Would you be willing to begin praying for God to provide you opportunities to minister to that person?

 Scripture memory verse for the week:

"For even the Son of Man came not to be served but to serve others and to give his life as a ransom for many." Matthew 20:28

 Prayer:

My Jesus, how beautiful, majestic, and holy you are! The heights of heaven cannot contain your glory! There is nothing in all creation beyond the reach of your power, your love, and your grace! And yet you willingly left all that behind to become Emmanuel – "God with us." You chose to live among our grime and tears and sweat and blood. You did that for me – for me – so that I could go into the world, to the hurting and poor and lost, and do it for them. I admit that I don't want ministry to be messy. I don't want my church or Sunday school class or worship service to become messy. If my heart is hardened about this, please soften it, Lord. If you could walk the road to Calvary, bearing the cruel cross of my own sinful messiness, can I do less for those around me? My life is no longer my own, but yours to command, so help me honor you by reaching out to those whom others ignore. Amen.

Notes & reflections

Week Eight:

Culture and the Kingdom

Read Acts 17, 18, & 19

In 2004, my family and I took our summer vacation along the northeastern seaboard of the United States. We went to Washington D.C., Baltimore, and New York City. We visited the monuments and the Smithsonian in Washington. We saw a baseball game and enjoyed Inner Harbor in Baltimore. And in New York we did a walking tour, took in a baseball game at old Yankee Stadium, and went to the top of the Empire State Building. For all of this I had mapped out a detailed itinerary so I would know where we were going in each city, and how much time we had.

We might think of Acts 17-19 as a travel itinerary. In these three chapters, Paul and his companions hit five different cities in about two years—Thessalonica, Berea, Athens, Corinth, and Ephesus. With the exception of Berea and Athens, the New Testament contains letters from Paul to the churches he planted in these cities. However, this was not just a travel itinerary to show how many Customs & Immigration stamps

Paul accumulated on his passport. It shows us the movement of the church and the advancement of God's kingdom through the work of the Holy Spirit.

Let's take note of several important things over the course of this two-year tour:

- *Paul always went to the local synagogues to persuade the Jews from the Scriptures that Jesus was the Christ (17:2, 10, 17; 18:4, 19; 19:8).* Intellectual and reasoned case for Jesus as the Christ and to explain the necessity of his death.
- *Paul and his companions faced constant persecution for doing so (17:5, 13, 32; 18:6, 17; 19:9, 29).*

- *In spite of these obstacles and difficulties, God continued to draw Jews and Gentiles into his kingdom through the missionary work of Paul and others (17:4, 11-12, 34; 18:8; 19:10, 18, 20).*

There is a wonderful passage in Acts 17:11 that can get overlooked if we are not careful. It reads, *"now the Berean Jews were of more noble character than those in Thessalonica, for they received the message with great eagerness and **examined the Scriptures every day** to see if what Paul said was true."* Did you notice that? They *examined the Scriptures every day.* These new converts spent quality time in God's Word on a regular basis. They took their newfound faith seriously and invested time in study so they would grow and mature.

A pastor friend of mine once said that we should be like the Bereans, searching the Scriptures with diligence, faith, and joy, in order to fully know and be obedient to Jesus. He challenged us not to simply take *his* word for something, but to study the scriptures ourselves. Pastors are human beings too, and we make mistakes just like everyone else. We do not seek to lead anyone astray or present incorrect information, but we may slip up and make mistakes. If listeners simply accept what a pastor says at face value — and it happens to be an instance where an error has been made — how will the listener know if he or she is not well grounded in the Word? Paul writes in Romans 3:3, *"Even if everyone else is a liar, God is true."* So while a pastor or teacher may err from time to time, God's revelation of himself in the Scriptures is always reliable.

Take a moment and reflect on how often you spend examining the Scriptures.

Do you simply take the pastor or Sunday school teacher's word about things, or do you explore it on your own? If not, how could you begin to do this on a consistent basis? How might a regular small group gathering aid you in searching the Scriptures?

The story of Paul in Athens (17:16-34) is extremely important for us as we seek to become more like the church in Acts. Take a moment to go back and re-read this section, paying special attention to how Paul used the Athenian culture to present the gospel.

Webster's New World College Dictionary defines culture as "the integrated pattern of human behavior that includes thought, speech, action, and artifacts and depends upon man's capacity for learning and transmitting knowledge to succeeding generations; the customary beliefs, social forms, and material traits of a racial, religious, or social group."[3] If we were fish, culture would be the water that we swim in. It is the things in our society that shape us, inform us, entertain us, and give definition to our lives. Television is part of our culture and has been for decades. We do not think much about it but it is there. Patriotism is part of our culture. Attending church is part of the Christian sub-culture.

In Athens, Paul used the Greek culture as a vehicle for sharing the gospel. *"Paul then stood up in the meeting of the Areopagus and said: "People of Athens! I see that in every way you are very religious. For as I walked around and looked carefully at your objects of worship..."* (17:22-23). While waiting for his traveling companions to join him in Athens, Paul spent some time "soaking up" the city. He took time to look and listen (...*as I walked around and looked carefully...*). So when he had the opportunity to formally present his arguments, he immediately used their own culture to his advantage.

"I see that in every way you are very religious." Paul recognized their culture's deep spirituality and commended them for it. He did not rant and bellow about idols, sinfulness, and God's wrath coming upon them for their false worship. He knew they took their religion(s) seriously.

"...I even found an altar with this inscription: TO AN UNKNOWN GOD." There were so many idols and temples in the city that Paul had discovered one to a "catch-all" deity. The Athenians did not know which god this was or what he/she did, but in order to make sure all their bases were covered, they felt this unknown god should have a nice altar, just like all the others did. Paul took this opening to explain about the

3   *Webster's New Collegiate Dictionary*, p.274

one true God in Jesus Christ.

In his message he also quoted Athenian literature: "*God did this so that they would seek him and perhaps reach out for him and find him, though he is not far from any one of us. 'For in him we live and move and have our being.' As some of your own poets have said, 'We are his offspring.'*" Paul had some knowledge of Greek poetry. He once again used the Athenian culture as a "carrier" for the good news.

Many Christians and churches believe that culture is bad, evil, and corrupt, and therefore should be avoided at all costs. Perhaps you have known someone reared in this sort of religious environment? People are forbidden to go to the movies, to listen to music (unless it is explicitly Christian), to wear make-up, to dress in certain styles, or to read certain books. They believe that by having as little to do with culture as possible, they can remain pure and holy. The problem with this perspective is that it is not biblical. How can we be *the light of the world* (Matthew 5:14) if we only shine on other Christians? How do we explain Paul's knowledge and use of Athenian literature if we are supposed to disengage from culture completely? The truth is, we cannot disengage from culture any more than a fish can stop swimming in water.

Others feel that we must embrace culture completely and fully. The motivation is noble: to try and reach people where they are, on their own turf, as we discussed in the previous devotion. But this approach can also be problematic. More often than not, the individual or church that embraces culture in this way ends up looking and acting no different than the culture. They have tried so hard to be cool or culturally acceptable that they have lost the distinctiveness of Christ. They are indistinguishable from the unsaved. If Paul had gone to Athens, started worshiping in all the temples, sacrificing to all the different gods, and behaving exactly like an Athenian, his witness would have been ruined. He would have looked just like everyone else.

So what are we to do with regard to culture? Too far one way and we are isolated, like the Amish. Too far the other way and we are compromised. The answer lies in finding a delicate balance between using the positive elements of culture, as Paul did in Athens, while avoiding the negative and destructive elements. The truth is that Jesus is not just interested in our souls. He is concerned about the whole of creation, including every culture on the planet. The church is called to help transform culture just as much as we are called to help transform lives. But in order to positively influence our culture, we must be knowledgeable about it. We need to know what we can and cannot use, how we can leverage the best of culture in order to advance the kingdom. But we must also be knowledgeable about God's Word. Studying and learning about our culture is important, but investment in the Scriptures is more so. Like the Bereans we discussed earlier, we need to saturate ourselves in God's Word to establish and maintain a solid foundation for our work in the world.

What are some positive aspects of our culture? What are some negative aspects? How has our culture changed since you were a child?

In what ways could your church leverage culture to help expand the kingdom?

Which way do most Christians lean

If Paul could speak to you right now, what do you think he would say about culture and God's Word?

In Acts 19:23-41 we see an example of how the gospel of Jesus Christ very often clashes with culture. Re-read that section again. The problem was the impact of the good news on economics (much like we saw in 16:16-19). Some of the craftsmen in Ephesus, who made money by selling idols, were angry about Paul's preaching, specifically "...[Paul] says that gods made by human hands are no gods at all" (19:26). Their lucrative lifestyle was in jeopardy. The craftsmen led a mob of such size "...the whole city was in an uproar" (19:29).

The gospel of grace and reconciliation runs contrary to much in our culture. The teachings of Jesus about money and possessions, about the poor, about loving and serving others, all fly in the face of the selfish, individualistic, greedy culture that we are a part of. The gospel shines light into the darkest aspects of our culture — not so we can stand back and tsk-tsk how bad it all is — but so that we can bring healing and restoration to the culture. Remember, God has no desire to destroy our culture; rather, he longs to redeem it so that it glorifies him.

How do you think money and material resources in our culture effects the church? What are some positive effects? What are some negative effects?

What elements of our culture would be the most difficult for you to do without? Why?

What are some cultural things around your church that Jesus might be calling your church to transform to his glory?

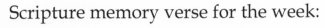

Scripture memory verse for the week:

Now the Bereans were of more noble character than those in Thessalonica, for they received the message with great eagerness and examined the Scriptures every day to see if what Paul said was true. Acts 17:11

Prayer:

Lord, help me to be open to your presence in the culture around me. Help me to see where you are at work, and how you are inviting me to join you in that work. Turn me away from the elements in culture that would harm me and hinder my relationship with you. Give me discernment and wisdom to know how to make use of culture to honor and glorify you. I believe that the growth you gave to the church in Acts can happen in my church, and I desire to be part of making it happen. Help yourself to me, Lord; humble me so that I may be the best instrument you have to reach the lost. Mold me, shape me, transform me, from the inside out, so that your holiness and love blaze forth in all I do and say. In the name of my blessed Deliverer and Shepherd, Jesus. Amen.

Notes & reflections

1) Last Macedonian King was defeated in 168 BC. Rome divided it into four districts with Thessalonica as the capital & Berea as the provincial assembly.

3rd Missionary Journey   Over 2500 miles

Week Nine:

Last Words

Read Acts 20, 21, & 22

21:17, End of Pauls 3rd missionary journey

When author was Radis...

One of the most difficult things I ever did in my ministry was saying goodbye to my youth group in 2005. I was preparing to step out of youth ministry and accept my first "solo" appointment as a pastor. I had served as youth pastor for five years, and had developed some deep and special friendships among the youth and adult leaders.

Knowing that the last Sunday of May would be the final time we would have together for our regular youth gathering, I planned something special. It could not be just another usual Sunday evening. I wanted to be able to say goodbye in a meaningful way. That is one thing we do not usually do well, saying goodbye. It is hard to say goodbye to people we love dearly. Sometimes we try to take shortcuts instead of fully entering into the grief of separation and departure. We think that if we avoid saying goodbye it will not hurt as much. But that is rarely ever the case.

I spent weeks preparing what we would do on our final

Sunday evening together. I had been reading about blessings in the Old Testament (Genesis 24:60; 27; 48:20; Numbers 6:22-27; Deuteronomy 15:4-6) and decided this would be the best way to say goodbye. I wrote up an individual blessing for every youth group member, specifically tailored to each one's personality, gifts, and dreams.

We met the final night and started with two games, then transitioned into a devotional time where we looked at a few of the Old Testament blessings. We talked about the purpose of a blessing and what it meant. I told them I would like to give each of them a personal blessing as the last thing I did as their youth pastor.

In a separate room I had set up a kneeling altar, candles, decorations, and ambient music. One by one each youth (and adult leader) came in and knelt at the altar rail. I anointed each one and gave them their blessing. Some of the junior high youth were easy to do since our relationship had not had a chance to develop very far. The older youth, however, broke my heart. I had been with them since seventh grade. After blessing one of my adult leaders, I remember hugging her, crying, and telling her "This is just *so hard*." It was much more difficult than I had expected.

After arriving at Miletus, Paul sent for the leaders of the church at Ephesus (20:17), a place where he lived for three years. This was the last time he would see them and he wanted to say goodbye. Paul's words to them (20:18-35) are his only recorded message to Christian believers in the book of Acts. All his other sermons, instructions, and arguments were directed toward Jew and Gentile non-believers.

What do you say at your final goodbye? What are your

last words?

Paul began by reminding them of where he had been. *"You know how I lived the whole time I was with you, from the first day I came into the province of Asia. I served the Lord with great humility and with tears and in the midst of severe testing by the plots of my Jewish opponents. You know that I have not hesitated to preach anything that would be helpful to you but have taught you publicly and from house to house. I have declared to both Jews and Greeks that they must turn to God in repentance and have faith in our Lord Jesus"* (20:18-21).

He told them of how he served among them; of the experiences they shared together, of the good times and the bad. He reminded them of how he preached everything they needed to hear — not just the happy, fluffy stuff to make them feel good — but every part of God's counsel. These elders of the church certainly knew how Paul had lived while he was among them. They had witnessed his humility, his work ethic, his compassion, and his fervor for the Lord. Now they were to do as he had done among them. Paul made this instruction even more explicit in his letter to the Corinthians when he wrote: *"And you should imitate me, just as I imitate Christ"* (1 Corinthians 11:1).

Next, he shared with them where he was going. *"And now, compelled by the Spirit, I am going to Jerusalem, not knowing what will happen to me there. I only know that in every city the Holy Spirit warns me that prison and hardships are facing me. However, I consider my life worth nothing to me; my only aim is to finish the race and complete the task the Lord Jesus has given me — the task of testifying to the good news of God's grace"* (20:22-24).

Paul was heading to Jerusalem. He seemed to know this

was his destiny, come what may, just as Jesus had likewise known his destiny awaited him in Jerusalem (Luke 9:51). Paul was fully prepared to face his own death there, again just like Jesus. The apostle's friends were not excited about this. They did not understand his commitment to this course of action (21:12-14). But Paul would not be dissuaded. He knew where he had to go. He might not have fully understood why at that point, but he was being faithful and obedient to God.

And third, Paul also knew where the church in Ephesus was going. This was what concerned him more than his own safety and well-being. *"Keep watch over yourselves and all the flock of which the Holy Spirit has made you overseers. Be shepherds of the church of God, which he bought with his own blood. I know that after I leave, savage wolves will come in among you and will not spare the flock. Even from your own number men will arise and distort the truth in order to draw away disciples after them. So be on your guard! Remember that for three years I never stopped warning each of you night and day with tears"* (20:28-31). There was trouble ahead; the church needed to be prepared for it. And it was up to the leaders, the shepherds, to exercise their authority and lead.

The Greek word translated as 'overseers' is *episkopos*. It refers to someone who has a definite function or a fixed purpose in a group. It is where we get our word 'episcopal.' These men, therefore, were the leaders of the church in Ephesus (probably of each individual house church gathering). Their responsibility was to 'shepherd' the church—that is, they were to be its guardians. Paul would later write to his young charge, Timothy, with requirements for anyone aspiring to the role of *episkopos*

(1 Timothy 3:1-7).

Before we conclude, let us take special notice of a few things in Paul's instructions to the church leaders. First, he says, "... *of which the Holy Spirit has made you overseers.*" Those who were chosen to lead the Ephesian church were not selected by popular vote, by family name, by the amount of money they had, or who spoke the loudest. The Holy Spirit chose these men for this task.

While human beings are swayed or intimidated by prestige, wealth, or larger-than-life antics, God is not. When choosing leaders for the church, we would do well to revisit 1 Samuel 16. God sent the prophet Samuel to Bethlehem to anoint King Saul's successor. As Jesse lined up his sons for review, Samuel was sure Israel's next king was right there in front of him. However, God told Samuel, "*Do not consider his appearance or his height, for I have rejected him. The LORD does not look at the things people look at. People look at the outward appearance, but the LORD looks at the heart*" (1 Samuel 16:7). When it became apparent that none of the young men standing before Samuel were God's chosen, Jesse, almost absentmindedly said, "Well, I do have one other son... But he's out in the fields tending the sheep." That "other son" was none other than David, who would go on to become the greatest king in the history of Israel.

We fall all over ourselves to elevate a person because of good looks, accomplishments, loud voice, or threat of reprisal. More often than not, the person is not the leader God has selected. God's criteria for leadership, as Samuel discovered that day in Bethlehem, is vastly different. The church would be more efficient, spiritual, and consistent if we allowed the

Spirit to choose men and women for leadership.

2   Second, the role of the Ephesian leaders was to shepherd or guard the church. They were not to do all the ministry of the church, nor were they to take over and create their own little kingdoms. They were responsible for steering, directing, and leading the church. The New Testament church operated through a horizontal system with all members being equal and all members being involved in the daily tasks of ministry. The pyramidal structure of leadership that we are familiar with developed in the wake of the legalization of Christianity in the Roman Empire. The church can only function in its God-designed fullness when all members are engaged in ministry and service, rather than relegating all of the work to a handful of trained professionals.

In addition, being a shepherd of the church meant these men had to be committed to their own spiritual growth, to accountability with other believers, to prayer, to the apostles' teaching, and most importantly, to Jesus. If they did these things, the evidence would be visible in their lives. The same is true for us today. Whether we have a position of leadership or not, we should likewise be committed to these disciplines. If we are not, the evidence will be visible in our lives (see Matthew 7:15-20). To exchange an inaccurate Constantinian model of church for the Acts model, we must be more diligent in who leads in our congregations. Those who show no interest in spiritual growth, discipleship, or obeying the commands of Christ should never be considered for leadership positions, regardless of how much money they claim to give or how many threats they issue.

3   Third, Paul noted "... *savage wolves will come in among* you..." He knew, from his own experiences of persecution at the hands of Jew and Gentile, that once he was no longer present and there was no chance of him returning, troublemakers would seize the opportunity. They would work to tear down the church in any way they could. Paul warned the leaders that they must remain vigilant against this external threat. The church, when it is operating in the power of the Holy Spirit and is fulfilling its mission and purpose can expect persecution from those outside. Tragically, that persecution can often come from other Christians.

And fourth, the apostle warned them *"Even from your own number men will arise and distort the truth..."* Once again, Paul understood that if the church leadership was not supportive of one another—if it was not strong, disciplined, and well-grounded in prayer—trouble would arise from the inside as well. There were those who would take advantage of opportunities to lead people astray. Paul even knew the reason or motivation for this kind of behavior: *"...in order to draw away disciples after them."* Within the church are those who will not hesitate to use deception to get their way, or who are so consumed with power and self-centeredness that they only desire to be in the spotlight. These warnings are firm and serious because Paul knew the fragility and vulnerability of the young Ephesian church.

Sadly, Paul's concern was well-founded. Revelation 2, written near the end of the first-century, some thirty years after Paul's death, records a warning from Jesus himself to the Ephesian church: *"Yet I hold this against you: You have forsaken the love you had at first. Consider how far you have fallen! Repent and do the things you did at first. If you do not repent, I will come to you and remove your lampstand from its place"* (2:4-5). The Ephesian church had drifted away from its main commitment to Jesus and his mission in the world. False teaching and compromise with the Roman culture around them had left the church in jeopardy.

These are warnings we still need to be vigilant about in our day. Persecution, bad theology, pop psychology, and other things seek to damage the church. Men and women within the church—who do not allow the Holy Spirit to transform their hearts and lives—manipulate, control, bully, and actively work to tear down anything they do not want. So Paul's last words to the elders of Ephesus still have meaning for us today, especially as we seek to help our churches return to their biblical roots.

What would you like to see your church be doing a year from now? Five years from now?

More young couples

How do Paul's instructions to the Ephesian elders compare to what we have already seen about the structure and ministry of the early church?

Have you ever held a leadership position in the church? If so, how did you feel about it? What did you like or dislike about it? Would you serve in a leadership position again, if asked? Why or why not?

Scripture memory verse for the week:

Care for the flock that God has entrusted to you. Watch over it willingly, not grudgingly — not for what you will get out of it, but because you are eager to serve God. Don't lord it over the people assigned to your care, but lead them by your own good example. 1 Peter 5:2-3

Prayer:

My Master and Savior, it is to you, and you alone, that I look to for my salvation, my peace, my joy, and my eternal hope. You are the One who has redeemed me for the special purpose and privilege of partnering with you in the work of your kingdom. If you call me to a position of leadership, let me trust that you have equipped me for that task. If I find myself trying to think up ways to avoid leadership, then challenge my heart. I fully understand that if every person in my church serves and ministers the way you have blessed them to, we will not be able to contain the growth you bring to us. If I have sat back and assumed that others will do all the hard work, please forgive me. If I have benefited from the ministry and service of others, show me how I can give back. I am yours, my Lord. I have surrendered my life into your hands, and I no longer live, but Christ lives in me. Let me serve for your glory and praise. Amen.

Notes & reflections

Week Ten:

Putting Convictions Before Convenience

Read Acts 23 and 24

Television courtroom programs have been around as long as television itself. From "Perry Mason" to "Night Court," "L.A. Law" to "Judge Judy," the viewing public has never been able to get enough legal drama (odd, considering the extravagant number of people involved in legal proceedings on any given day…). Along with police procedurals and the medical setting, the courtroom rounds out the top three backdrops for television storytelling. If you happen to be a fan of legal dramas on television, chances are good you will enjoy Acts 23-26.

Chapter twenty-three finds Paul before the Sanhedrin—the Jewish supreme court—on (false) charges of teaching against the Law of Moses and defiling the temple. Paul got off on the wrong foot with the high priest (23:2-5), but rescued himself and took advantage of the differences among the religious-political groups within the Sanhedrin. This would be like us pitting Democrats and Republicans against each other. All it took was a little prodding — *"I stand on trial because of the hope of the resurrection of the dead"* (23:6) — and something resembling a brawl erupted.

This led to a devious plot to ambush Paul and do him in. It is interesting how these loyal, faithful, law-abiding Jews were more than willing to break their own law *("...We have taken a solemn oath not to eat anything until we have killed Paul.")* in order to get rid of Paul. This should tell us a great deal about the condition of their hearts and their commitment to God. Whenever we are willing to reject or ignore the commands of God for our own convenience or satisfaction, we are in a bad spot. However, the plot came to light (did you really think forty guys could keep something like that a secret?), and with the help of some Roman soldiers, Paul was transferred from Jerusalem to Caesarea.

Jesus said, *"When you are brought before synagogues, rulers and authorities, do not worry about how you will defend yourselves or what you will say, for the Holy Spirit will teach you at that time what you should say"* (Luke 12:11-12). This is exactly what happened to Paul. His case was brought before Felix, the governor over Israel. We are told that Felix *"...was well acquainted with the Way"* (24:22) and was therefore more than a bit sympathetic toward Paul. *He ordered the centurion to keep Paul under guard but* **to give him some freedom** *and* **permit his friends to take care of his needs** (24:23).

We do not know where or how Felix came to his knowledge of the Way, but it was apparent he wanted to know more from Paul. *"As Paul talked about righteousness, self-control and the judgment to come, Felix was afraid and said, 'That's enough for now! You may leave. When I find it convenient, I will send for you'"*

(24:25). It is obvious that Paul did not alter or water down the message of the gospel just because Felix had shown him some comfort, nor because he was a high-ranking official. The gospel is for everyone and does not allow favoritism. It is no wonder Felix became uncomfortable the more Paul talked about righteousness and self control: the governor had neither when he lured Drusilla, his wife, away from her former husband, King Aziz of Emesa. This (and the other sins he had committed, for Felix was known as a tyrannical and unjust governor) put him squarely under divine judgment. He would not repent, but did continue to interview Paul. At that point he was not seeking to learn more about faith in Christ. *"...he was hoping that Paul would offer him a bribe, so he sent for him frequently and talked with him"* (24:26).

Bribery was illegal according to Roman law, but that did not stop it from being a rather common practice. Particularly in the more remote provinces of the empire, things happened more smoothly if the wheels of government were oiled from time to time with judicious bribes. However, Paul had no intention of doing this. Felix may have assumed that because Paul *"...came to Jerusalem to bring my people gifts for the poor and to present offerings"* (24:17), he had access to significant funds. But Paul himself probably had little, if any, money by this time.

A bribe would likely have gotten Paul released, or at least transferred somewhere so he could be released. But the apostle would not compromise his convictions for the sake of convenience. He would not take the shortcut that was being offered.

Often when we face trials or difficulties, we look for the

quickest way out of them. While this may be a natural reaction, it may actually work *against* what God has planned for us and for others. Because Paul was walking so faithfully in the Holy Spirit, God had already told him, *"Take courage! As you have testified about me in Jerusalem, so you must also testify in Rome"* (23:11). Paul knew his destiny was no longer tied to Jerusalem, as was his Lord's; rather, Paul's destiny would take him to the seat of world power, the heart of the empire. If he had tried to bribe Felix and avoid imprisonment—if he was interested in making his life easier—he would have been sabotaging what God planned to use him for in Rome.

But pay attention to the length of Paul's imprisonment: *"When **two years** had passed…"* (24:27). Two years! Paul was incarcerated for 24 months. Even though he had a few freedoms during that time, he was nonetheless a prisoner. It makes you stop and wonder if Paul ever questioned this lengthy delay in his ministry? I know I would have been climbing the walls, thinking about all the wonderful opportunities I was missing out on. And perhaps Paul had similar thoughts on occasion. But I believe he also came to recognize all this was part of God's plan. There were opportunities for him to share the faith with Felix and Drusilla, as well as others in the governor's palace. Sometimes the very place we *do not* want to be is the place we *most need to be* in God's grand design.

There is another biblical character that would certainly have had sympathy for Paul's situation. His name was Joseph. During this week, take some time and read four chapters in Genesis (37, 39 - 41). Look at the suffering and injustice Joseph endured. Think about the feelings and questions he must have had. Think about all the opportunities probably

said no the potiphars' wife

presented to Joseph to compromise his convictions in order to make his situation easier.

We cannot know all that God has planned for the church or us. His divine will for us may involve difficulties, hardship, sacrifice, and discomfort. The question is: will we compromise our convictions to avoid those things? Will we take shortcuts so that our comforts, entitlements, and conveniences are not upset? Or will we be like Joseph and Paul — patiently waiting and trusting that God's plans *"...works for the good of those who love him, who have been called according to his purpose"* (Romans 8:28)?

Once we compromise our convictions — once we give in and sell our integrity away just to stay happy or content — we no longer stand for anything of significance. As the old sayings go, "If you don't stand for something you'll fall for anything," and "Character is who you are when everyone is looking, and who you are when no one is looking."

Can you think of a time when you compromised something you believed in for the sake of convenience? How do you feel about that now?

What happened to Joseph as a result of his refusal to take shortcuts and avoid inconvenience and injustice? What happened to Egypt? What happened to his family?

What are some ways a church might compromise its convictions for the sake of convenience?

By not taking a stand on social issues?

Scripture memory verse for the week:

Let your eyes look straight ahead; fix your gaze directly before you. Give careful thought to the paths for your feet and be steadfast in all your ways. Do not turn to the right or the left; keep your foot from evil. Proverbs 4:25-27

Prayer:

Heavenly Father, my world offers me so many opportunities to compromise what I believe. I am surrounded by deception and encouraged to embrace what you have said is wrong. Make me strong in spirit, Father, that I may honor you with integrity and faithfulness. Even though I cannot comprehend all your ways for my church and me, I nevertheless renew my trust in your goodness. Help me to encourage those who are struggling, and to offer words of hope and comfort. Regardless of the pain or persecution I may experience, let me be as true to you as Joseph and Paul were. In Christ's name. Amen.

Notes & reflections

_____

_____

_____

_____

_____

_____

_____

Dec 1

Week Eleven:

Tell the Story

Read Acts 25 and 26

While studying in seminary, my family and I lived near Lexington, Kentucky. While there we discovered the fervor and passion of University of Kentucky basketball. No matter where I went I could always count on hearing someone talking about UK sports. The same can be said about any college or university sports program, or any professional sports franchise. Each one has dedicated fans that know all about their team and love talking about them.

We also hear lots of talk today about the latest must-see film, the video that has gone viral, the price of gasoline, the latest singer or dancer who got bounced from a television program, goofy celebrity shenanigans, and of course, politics.

But for some reason we do not hear a lot of talk about our faith journeys, as individuals and as churches. It seems that most Christians, at least those of the more non-charismatic tribes, have lost the desire or ability to tell their faith stories. We know a little about the people we worship with. We know where they work, which restaurants they like or do not like, and who their family members are. But we do not know their faith journeys very well. If we do not hesitate to talk to one another about ball games and cars and recipes and community events, why are we so reluctant to talk about the Lord? Paul certainly was not shy about it.

The apostle's legal battle continued. In chapter twenty-five, new governor Festus was approached by the religious establishment and Jewish leaders, petitioning him to move Paul's trial to Jerusalem. They were planning another attempt on Paul's life. Festus was not interested in all the hassle and time involved in commuting the trial, so he told the Jews to come to Caesarea and present their charges there.

They did. And as the hearing was underway, "*Festus, wishing to do the Jews a favor, said to Paul, 'Are you willing to go up to Jerusalem and stand trial before me there on these charges?'*" (25:9). The new governor wanted to get off on the right foot with the Sanhedrin by making this offer. If Paul accepted, the political machinery of Rome and Israel would be greased further. But unfortunately for Festus, Paul did not accept. Instead, "*I appeal to Caesar!*" (25:11) was his reply.

Every Roman citizen had the right to appeal his or her case to a higher court in Rome. Paul, being a Roman citizen, was well aware of the law. He knew that if his trial was held in Jerusalem, powerful local forces might possibly override Roman law. Paul was also surely thinking about the word he had received from the Lord, "*Take courage! As you have testified about me in Jerusalem, so you must also testify in Rome*" (23:11). The path of his destiny and witness to Jesus was leading him toward Rome, not Jerusalem.

Before Paul could be sent to Rome for his appeal, Festus needed to prepare a statement of the formal charges against the apostle. *"But I have nothing definite to write to His Majesty about him"* (25:26). So he solicited the help of visiting dignitary King Agrippa. Festus was at a loss as to how to proceed. If Paul was sent to Rome without formal charges, Festus would look incompetent. On the other hand, the governor did not really know how to document the Jewish charges against Paul. Perhaps King Agrippa, having a substantial understanding of Jewish law and religion, could help?

It is at this point where we once again see Paul fearlessly tell his conversion story. This is the story that so many Christians are reluctant to share. Each of us has a testimony if we are a follower of Jesus Christ. Some may be more dramatic than others (such as Paul's), but drama is not a requirement for having a testimony. A relationship with Jesus Christ is the only requirement. There are three elements in a testimony we must recapture and be willing to share, just as Paul was.

The first is **where we were and who we were before Jesus Christ.** Paul began his defense by looking back at where he had come from. *"The Jewish people all know the way I have lived ever since I was a child, from the beginning of my life in my own country, and also in Jerusalem. They have known me for a long time and can testify, if they are willing, that I conformed to the strictest sect of our religion, living as a Pharisee"* (26:4-5). He continued to share about his past up through verse eleven.

We were all *somewhere* before we came to Jesus Christ. We all had a sinful past. We were not living according to God's commands. We were separated from God and most likely had no clue, nor did we care, about God. We were trapped in sin and rebellion. In order to share our story, we have to start with our brokenness, sinfulness, and self-centeredness. We do not want to give the devil too much credit for that time in our lives, so there is no need to go into a lot of detail. We never want to glorify our sinful past. But it is important to let others know that our lives were not what they should have been. Paul gives us an excellent example of how to do this.

The second element of our testimony is **how we came to know and receive Jesus Christ into our lives.** For Paul, this was his "Damascus Road experience." *"On one of these journeys I was going to Damascus with the authority and commission of the chief priests. About noon, King Agrippa, as I was on the road, I saw a light from heaven, brighter than the sun, blazing around me and my companions. We all fell to the ground, and I heard a voice saying to me in Aramaic, 'Saul, Saul, why do you persecute me? It is hard for you to kick against the goads.' Then I asked, 'Who are you, Lord?' 'I am Jesus, whom you are persecuting,' the Lord replied"* (26:12-15).

There was a turning point in our lives when we fully realized and accepted the love, forgiveness, and grace of Jesus Christ. We turned our backs on our old sinful lifestyle with its destructive, God-hating habits, and chose to walk and live in the power of the Holy Spirit. This moment should have completely and totally transformed our lives.

The third element is **what God has done for us since we accepted Christ into our lives**. The Lord told Paul ..."*Now get up and stand on your feet. I have appeared to you to appoint you as a servant and as a witness of what you have seen and will see of me. I will rescue you from your own people and from the Gentiles. I am sending you to them to open their eyes and turn them from dark-*

ness to light, and from the power of Satan to God, so that they may receive forgiveness of sins and a place among those who are sanctified by faith in me" (26:16-18). This was Paul's commission for the work he would do for Christ. Nothing would ever be the same again for the Jew from Cilicia.

Scripture tells us in several places that we are to proclaim all the things God has done. Consider this passage from Psalm 71:15-18: *"I will tell everyone about your righteousness. All day long I will proclaim your saving power, though I am not skilled with words. I will praise your mighty deeds, O Sovereign LORD. I will tell everyone that you alone are just. O God, you have taught me from my earliest childhood, and I constantly tell others about the wonderful things you do. Now that I am old and gray, do not abandon me, O God.*

Let me proclaim your power to this new generation, your mighty miracles to all who come after me."

Our testimonies do not always have to be a life story. They can be about God's presence and faithfulness during an illness or a time of grief. They can be about something that happened yesterday. They can be about struggles, doubts, or questions that God has brought us through. As David said, even though *I am not skilled with words*, we still have the privilege and responsibility to share our personal story, inside and outside the church.

Doing so binds us together in the church. When we share our God-stories, we are less likely to be distracted by or drawn into gossip, judgment, pride, or greed. A Christ-centered testimony has great power to build up, encourage, unify, bless, and praise — all things which Satan does not want us to do. In fact, Satan has a significant reason for not wanting us to share our God-stories. In Revelation 12:11 we read, *"They triumphed over [Satan]* **by the blood of the Lamb** *and* **by the word of their testimony."** Whenever we open our mouths to declare the victory and triumph of God in our lives, we turn the tables on the devil!

It is important that we practice talking to one another about our faith. The world cannot take away our testimony. It is uniquely ours, and yet each one is different because God has worked differently in all of us. But the world very often will not understand or will reject our faith stories. As Paul came to the end of his defense, Festus interrupted him: *"'You are out of your mind, Paul!' he shouted. 'Your great learning is driving you insane'"* (26:24). The governor thought Paul had spent so much time with his head buried in theology books that he was now a candidate for the nuthatch! Yet again we see persecution come against Paul because of his faith.

But pay attention to how Paul handled this door God opened for him: *"'I am not insane, most excellent Festus,' Paul replied. 'What I am saying is true and reasonable. The king is familiar with these things, and I can speak freely to him. I am convinced that none of this has escaped his notice, because it was not done in a corner. King Agrippa, do you believe the prophets? I know you do.' Then Agrippa said to Paul, 'Do you think that in such a short time you can persuade me to be a Christian?' Paul replied, 'Short time or long – I pray to God that not only you but all who are listening to me today may become what I am, except for these chains'"* (26:25-29).

The great apostle seized the opportunity being set before him. Knowing that King Agrippa had knowledge of the Jewish scriptures, and that he believed in them, Paul appealed to the king for understanding — and perhaps agreement. Agrippa was not keen about being put on the spot, so he dodged Paul's question with a lighthearted, "Why, Paul, are you trying to convert me?" Actually, yes, he was! Paul told the entire assembly that he wished they knew Jesus Christ and could share in what Paul offered.

I love the fact that Paul simply let things rest after that. He did not try to force King Agrippa to "make a decision." He did not give an altar call, nor did he continue to talk on and on. He fully trusted that the Holy Spirit had already been at work, and remained at work, in those who heard him. Paul was humble enough to realize the outcome did not depend on him, and trusting enough that the Holy Spirit would work all things out. When we are given opportunities to share our testimonies with those outside the church, it is not up to us to convince or convert them. As we have already said, that is the job of the Holy Spirit. We are to merely be faithful to say what God has done for us and in us through Jesus Christ.

When was the last time you shared your faith journey with another person? Describe what happened.

Couple weeks ago the construction, woke told him how I ran from God for a lot of years. He said he is running, his wife is a christian

Why do you think many Christians are reluctant to share their testimonies? *Fear of you'll be looked at Fear of Intellectual Debate*

Take some time this week to write down your testimony. Include the three elements mentioned in this section.

Set aside one Sunday school class gathering every few weeks and use the time to share your faith stories together.

Can you think of one person in your sphere of influence that could benefit from hearing about what the Lord has done for you? Would you begin to pray that God would give you an opportunity to share your story?

How might sharing our testimonies with each other help our church become healthier? How might they help your church to grow?

Scripture memory verse for the week:

We proclaim to you what we have seen and heard, so that you also may have fellowship with us. And our fellowship is with the Father and with his Son, Jesus Christ. We write this to make our joy complete. 1 John 1:3-4

Prayer:

Savior and Master, I am so grateful to you for giving me a testimony of your faithfulness, grace, peace, and hope. Help me to share it willingly and joyfully. Bring people into my path that need to hear how good you are, and what you long to do in their lives. If I am timid, grant me courage to speak about you. If I am shy, grant me intimacy with the ones I share with. And Lord, if it be your will, please use my story to draw others into your precious kingdom. Amen.

Notes & reflections

Week Twelve:

Fulfilling the Mission of Jesus Christ

Read Acts 27 and 28

We have reached the end of the story of the early church, at least as recorded in Acts. Through the letters in the New Testament we can glean a few other aspects of the early church's life and work.

So what do we do now? Close the Bible, file the devotional away on a shelf, and continue to conduct "church as usual"?

Not for me. And I hope not for you, either.

The mission of the church is the same now as it was in Acts 1:8 — *"But you will receive power when the Holy Spirit comes on you; and you will be my witnesses in Jerusalem, and in all Judea and Samaria, and to the ends of the earth."* We are responsible for living out this command. It is not optional. We are called and set apart to be an alternative community that shows the world what the kingdom of God looks like in real, practical, and tangible ways. We are to carry on the mission and work of Jesus. What Jesus did, we are to do. Where Jesus went, we are to go. What it cost Jesus, it will cost us.

Chapter twenty-eight ends with these two sentences: *"For two whole years Paul stayed there in his own rented house and welcomed all who came to see him. He proclaimed the kingdom of God and taught about the Lord Jesus Christ — with all boldness and without hindrance!"* (28:30-31). You might have noticed that we never get to see Paul's defense before Caesar. We have no idea what he said or what happened. All we are told to end the chronicle of the early church is that Paul kept on teaching. Now why would Luke stop the story just like that? We are all left hanging, wondering what happened at Paul's trial.

The reason for such a conclusion is simple: *the story of the church is not over!* Paul's trial before Caesar was not the end of the story. Luke specifically ended Acts this way so the church would know the mission was still incomplete. Just because Paul made it to Rome — *the ends of the earth* — did not mean the mission of Jesus was finished. Not at all! In fact, ever since the end of Acts, the church has been living in Acts 29. "Sure," you may say, "but there is no Acts 29." That is true. We do not have a 29th chapter *in our Bible*, but we do have a 29th chapter around us every single day. Jesus expects us to follow in his footsteps, to love how he loved, to reach people with the gospel, and to make disciples of them (Matthew 28:19-20).

I hope you have been able to see and understand why we need to reclaim the identity and heritage we have studied about in Acts. We need to move away from man-made structures and systems. We need to stop thinking of the church, and running the church, like a business or a family reunion. I am not advocating that we tear down our buildings, sell off our land, or recycle our hymnals. But I am suggesting that we take a serious, concentrated look at our churches and compare them to what we have seen in Acts. It is time for a movement of God's people back to the essence of the early church. We have not been redeemed, restored, gifted, and called so that we can prop up a dying institution. We need to re-orient our eyes, hearts, and spirits upon the task of reaching the world for the glory of God.

But some will say, "We can't reach the whole world! We're not smart enough; we don't have enough resources; we don't have enough people. We simply can't do it." And in one sense, those voices would be right. *We* can't.

BUT. . .

GOD. . .

CAN.

Take a moment and think back over what you have discovered in Acts. How much of the early church's ministry was accomplished through human power, ingenuity, and design?

None. It only happened because of prayer and the Holy Spirit.

How many people came to Christ because of the eloquence of the apostles' preaching?

None. It only happened because of prayer and the Holy Spirit. Some scholars believe that Paul was not a tremendously gifted or eloquent speaker. This would seem to be borne out when we consider 2 Corinthians 10:10, *For some say, "His letters are weighty and forceful, but in person he is unimpressive and his speaking amounts to nothing."*

How much of the early church's growth was dependent upon the Christians' planning, creativity, and events?

None. It only happened because of prayer and the Holy Spirit.

Do you see the pattern?

God's desire is to be glorified throughout the whole world, and to have the name of Jesus known all across the globe. If that is what God wants, it makes sense to assume he will do whatever it takes to make it happen. You see it is not up to us. On our own, we cannot, or will not, do it. But if the church is willing to partner with God, to see where the Father is at work and join him there, we can be part of his redeeming and transforming work.

Throughout this study we have witnessed several components that were vital to the early church, and which must become vital for us again today. If we surrender our man-made traditions and controls, and willingly embrace these four things, our churches will not be able to contain all that God has for us!

The first of these is **the power and presence of the Holy Spirit:** Acts 1:4-5, 8; 2:1-4, 15-21, 33, 38; 4:8, 31; 5:3, 32; 6:3, 5, 10; 7:51, 55; 8:15-17, 29; 9:17, 31; 10:44-45, 47; 11:12, 15-16, 24, 28; 13:2, 4, 9, 52; 15:8, 28; 16:6-7; 19:2, 6; 20:22-23; 21:4, 11; 28:25.

If this is a bit redundant, that is okay. We need to hear this again and again. Without the power and presence of the Holy Spirit, everything we do is of human origin. We may be able to accomplish good worship services or outreach events, but God does not want what is *good* for us. He wants what is *best* for us. Too many churches settle for what is good because it is safe, predictable, and non-threatening, rather than pursue the greater things God has for us.

What would you be willing to give up so that your church might experience more of the power and presence of

the Holy Spirit?

How would you say your church settles for what is good
instead of what is best?

How would you feel if the Holy Spirit started doing in
your church what we have seen him do in Acts?

The second component is **prayer:** Acts 1:14, 24; 2:42; 3:1;
4:24, 31; 6:6; 8:15; 9:40-10:9, 19-20; 12:5, 12; 13:3; 16:13, 16, 25;
20:36; 21:5; 22:17; 28:8.

Most churches today do not prioritize prayer. It is treated
as an add-on, something to jump-start committee meetings
with. So much of what we seek to accomplish is actually being done under our own power and plans. The Holy Spirit is
rarely allowed to work and move with full freedom.

We tend to get skittish if the Spirit shows up. We know
he may do things we do not want or refuse to accept; he may
call us to change our behaviors or attitudes; he may be seeking to lead the church somewhere we do not want it to go.
So we pat the Holy Spirit on the head, briefly acknowledge
his presence, and then go on with our agendas. We remain
ineffective, isolated, and irrelevant because we want to keep
the church operating in a Roman/Constantinian model rather
than a New Testament model.

Prayers offered up only once or twice on Sunday mornings, and once during a meeting, simply are not enough. In
order for us to accomplish the mission of Jesus Christ, we

need times for faithful prayer warriors to meet and intercede together for the world, the church, and its mission. We need prayer time before worship, before outreach and mission activities, before and during meetings. Without such commitment to prayer, we will continue to falter, lack power, and struggle to make a difference.

List three people you know who you could approach about starting an ongoing prayer group. When will you contact them?

Make a list of three areas within your church that you need to begin praying for: *Leadership*

2) The third element is **small groups:** Acts 1:3-6; 2:1, 42-46; 5:12, 42; 18:2-3, 26; 20:7-9, 20.

Jesus surrounded himself with twelve men who shared in his life and ministry. There were others who followed him, but only the Twelve had the "inside track" with Jesus. He was training them to carry on his mission after he was gone. Let us also remember how Jesus spent considerably more time with Peter, James, and John. Of the Twelve, three had an even deeper relationship with the Lord. As we have seen in Acts and church history, until the legalization of Christianity by the Roman Empire, the church did its best work through small groups.

Small groups provide more intimate opportunities for people to learn and share their faith. In the small group, people get to know one another — their needs, struggles, hopes, and questions — in ways that deepen the bonds between them. As they share their lives together, spiritual maturity takes hold and grows. In addition, participants learn to identify, develop, and apply their spiritual giftedness. Through a commitment to small group discipleship, we are trained for evangelism and witness in a smaller, less threatening space. Those who love, support and encourage us help keep us accountable to the Lord.

The small group also leads to effective church growth. George G. Hunter III, in his book *Radical Outreach: The Recovery of Apostolic Ministry & Evangelism* says, "Churches grow larger by growing smaller. That is, as the church multiples small groups and other small faith-sharing communities, and as it involves more and more of its people in small groups, and as it involves seekers in small groups before they ever believe or commit, and as its increasing numbers of small groups are reaching out to more and more pre-Christian people, those dynamics substantially contribute to the growth of the church."[4]

The Methodist movement began as a series of small group meetings.

John Wesley referred to them as "classes." They were weekly gatherings, overseen by a lay leader, wherein each person reported to the group on their progress in sanctification through worship, the sacraments, study, prayer, and service. Members were held accountable to their walk of faith. Small groups, which up to that point had dwindled off in

4   Radical Outreach: The Recovery of Apostolic Ministry & Evangelism, George G. Hunter III (Abingdon Press, Nashville, 2003; pp. 115-116)

significance in the church, helped carry Wesley's Methodist renewal movement.

How would you feel about taking part in a weekly small group?

Who in your church do you think would be good small group leaders? Would you be willing to approach one of these people and ask him or her to begin a group that you could be part of?

The fourth component is **going / being sent/ becoming missional and incarnational**: Acts 1:8; 8:1, 4, 14, 26; 9:32; 11:19-20, 22; 13:3-4, 5-6, 13-14, 51; 14:8, 20, 21, 24-25; 15:3, 22, 39-41; 16:6, 8, 10-12; 17:1, 10, 14-15; 18:1, 18, 22-23; 19:1, 21; 20:1-3, 6; 21:1-3, 7; 22:21; 23:11; 27:24.

The church should always be focused outward. As we have noted previously, we are to be incarnational. We are to become Christ for those lost in the darkness. We are to go to them just as Christ came to us. When we fail to go and meet people where they are, we fail Christ. If all we do is expect people to show up at our nice buildings on Sunday morning (the attractional mode), we are not operating as the church.

Going requires prayer, perseverance, compassion, and a spiritual hunger to see people drawn to Jesus. The more churches move beyond themselves to touch the world, the more God takes care of the needs within the church. The more Christians are willing to become missional, to think and act like missionaries in their neighborhoods and communities, the more our churches will grow. People of the twenty-first century will not come to our worship services simply because we are having them. Those days, as wonderful as they may have been, are gone. It is time for the church to leave its buildings, classrooms, and sanctuaries, and engage in ministry where the needs are the greatest. It is risky, challenging, messy, and often difficult. It is what we have seen repeatedly throughout Acts.

What are some ways you and another church member could begin to be more missional and incarnational?

Re-read some of the Acts passages listed above. Which ones stand out and speak the strongest to you. What do you think God is saying to you in these passages?

Scripture memory verse for the week:

"For I know the plans I have for you," declares the LORD, "plans to prosper you and not to harm you, plans to give you hope and a future. Then you will call on me and come and pray to me, and I will listen to you. You will seek me and find me when you seek me with all your heart." Jeremiah 29:11-13

Prayer:

Glorious Father, all-powerful Son, blessed Holy Spirit — thank you for speaking to me during my study of Acts. I have learned much; but I know this has not simply been so I could accumulate more knowledge. You have been preparing me to help my church live in Acts 29 time. I recognize that you have something special for me to do in helping your kingdom to become real to others. I am willing to surrender whatever stands in your way — whatever I cling to or demand or think the world owes me — so that you may use me to your glory. If my church is to change, I ask that you change me first, Father. Show me the vision and hope you have for your church, and may I be so captivated by it that I will do whatever it takes to make it happen. I pray for all the others who have made this devotional journey with me, that their faith walk has been challenged and has grown deeper. Draw all of us together to transform your church from a stale institution to a vibrant movement that fulfills the mission of Jesus Christ! It is in his radiant and supreme name that I make this prayer. Amen.

Notes & reflections

Back to the Beginning

It is my prayer that this devotional has been a blessing to you and has challenged you in how you look at the church. As we have seen throughout Acts, whenever the church steps out in the power of the Holy Spirit, persecution soon follows. Satan has no interest in watching the church move forward, bring people to Jesus Christ, and make them into faithful disciples. Regretfully, the Prince of Lies has a great many churches right where he wants them: apathetic, spiritually shallow, ingrown, and with no sense of mission or purpose. However, as soon as the church steps out in faith and trust, amazing things begin to happen. Your journey through Acts should have made this abundantly clear.

I deeply enjoyed my time of study, meditation, prayer, and writing as this book came together. I have encountered new insights and am more convinced than ever that the future of the church lies in reclaiming our New Testament heritage and roots. The model of church that has been in existence for 1,800 years has done much good. God has used his church in a myriad of ways to declare the glories of Jesus Christ across the globe. But far too many churches, in far too many places, function more like museums or funeral parlors than the living, active body of Christ. That is because we have allowed a human system of rules and leadership, drawn from the Roman civil arena, to take the place of the Holy Spirit.

We are more interested in keeping big givers happy and contributing than with going into the heart of the darkness with the light of Christ. Due to the influence of our culture and society, we are more interested in raising bigger buildings than in raising up faithful disciples. We have expected a handful of professionals (and a few stalwart volunteers) to manage all the work and ministry of the church, but many of us have done little or nothing to contribute positively. We have been more focused on what each individual person wants or does not want, rather than on what the helpless and dying all around us need. We have used our God-given finances and resources to live more and more luxuriously, while the majority of the world lives in grinding poverty. We have chosen to accept certain teachings of Jesus, but reject those that call us to change, to share, and to serve.

I hope this devotional has pricked something within you. I hope the Holy Spirit has been speaking powerfully and regularly to you. And I sincerely hope you have been listening. If we want to see the mission of Jesus Christ fulfilled, it is only going to happen when you and I decide that it is time to stop "playing church."

The time has come to stop choosing leaders because "We don't want to hurt anyone's feelings by not nominating them." We likewise need to replace leaders whose actions and words reveal no heart or desire to act as servants. I have often told my congregations, "If you can't clean a toilet as an act of service for someone, you have no business being in a church leadership position."

It is time to stop assuming that God has a limited amount of resources available to any given church. We must do away with the "mentality of scarcity." It is unbiblical. We should desire to stop spending money *inside* the building and start spending it *outside* the building. And no, that does not mean on church landscaping or a new parking lot! It means on those who are in need. It is time we quit worrying about what someone else says or thinks about who goes to the altar. And please, let us do away with the assumption that large attendance numbers equals a healthy church.

Attendance and giving are the two worst criteria for assessing the spiritual health of a church. They happen to be the quickest and easiest to measure, and we are all about quick and easy, aren't we? But those figures mean nothing if the church is spiritually dead. Better an attendance of forty Spirit-filled, radical Jesus followers who want to turn the world upside down than four hundred who are there to treat the body of Christ like a social club.

If these things resonate with you — if your heart beats faster at the prospect of watching the Holy Spirit have free reign in your church — then consider some of these suggestions as your next steps:

(1) If you are a pastor, go back and slowly work your way through Acts. Take note of the differences between the early church and the institution we have today. Ask the Holy Spirit to reveal the preferred future he has for your congregation. Surround yourself with like-minded believers who can support, guide, and champion a transition into a more Christ-centered, Spirit-led movement. This will not be easy and it will take time. You will incur the wrath of those who are content with their comforts and control. You may even risk losing your job. But as you study Acts, bear in mind the persecution and obstacles the early believers faced in order to fulfill the mission of Jesus.

If you are a lay person, begin praying about what God would have you do. Arrange a meeting with your pastor and key church leaders and talk with them about what you have discovered while going through Acts. Do not, under any circumstances, try to go around your pastor. He or she is the leader God has placed over your congregation. If the pastor is resistant to change or turnaround, do not push it. You can still gather with other church members for small group interaction, and can carry out the mission of Jesus Christ that way.

If your pastor and church leaders are supportive, let them know you will stand with them in whatever ways are necessary. They need to know that you will be there for them through thick and thin. If you are serious about this, you too will encounter resistance and opposition from those in your fellowship.

(2) Begin a small group meeting. Remember, the early church met in homes, in small group gatherings. There were no large sanctuaries or educational buildings or family life centers like we have today. Invite a few friends who are willing to commit one-and-a-half to two hours per week meeting together for prayer, worship, Bible study, and missions/ outreach. There are plenty of good books available on the dynamics of small groups.

(3) Begin a prayer gathering. Set aside a designated time each week (or each day, if your church is big enough and has enough willing servants), and meet together for the specific purpose of prayer. Place a map of the world in your prayer room. Label it with missionaries and ministries your church supports. Keep a list of upcoming church activities in the room to be prayed over. You should also have information available so people can pray for the pastor and church staff, for needs in the community, for worship services, and for the vision and mission of the church. Be faithful to this date and time, and remain consistent in prayer.

(4) Set up a pre-worship prayer time. Worship services should be *bathed* in prayer. Arrange for a group of committed servants who will arrive before the scheduled worship time and pray specifically for the service, the pastor, choir and musicians, congregation members, and visitors. This group should also set aside a few minutes before the service begins to lay hand on and pray for the pastor. Speaking from personal experience, when this has been done for me, I am more energized and confident. When it has not been done for me, I find myself in the same old rut week after week. Again, this must be done faithfully and consistently.

(5) Establish a visitor follow-up taskforce. Some people in the church have a great gift of reaching out and making people feel welcome. Have these individuals do weekly follow-up with visitors who attend worship, Bible studies, or outreach events. In our twenty-first century society, people respond more positively to *church members* who visit them. They want to know if the people of the church *really* and *truly* care for them and want them. Pastors or elders can follow up when needed.

(6) **Help train your congregation about spiritual gifts.** According to Scripture, every believer in Christ has also received the Holy Spirit, and the Spirit gives spiritual gifts. These gifts are for the edifying and building up of the church. Congregations who do not know their spiritual gifts, or who have no interest in spiritual gifts, generally wear the pastor and staff out. These church members expect and demand that all ministries be done to them or for them. This is unbiblical, inconsiderate, selfish, and unfair. For churches to reclaim their New Testament roots, members will have to learn their spiritual gifts and begin to function in them. There are many books and online resources available to help learn and teach about spiritual gifts. An excellent way to begin a small group gathering is by spending a few weeks together studying what the Bible teaches about spiritual gifts, and the role of every member of the body of Christ.

(7) **Include times for personal testimonies in worship on a regular basis.** At the church I pastor, once a month we have someone share his or her testimony in both of our worship services. Most church members are surprised to discover aspects of their friends' spiritual journeys they never knew before. Again, if you are a layperson, be sure your pastor and worship leaders are on board with this. And do not dump it on the pastor, worship leader, or administrative assistant to find someone each time. You take that responsibility.

(8) **Spread the gospel by increasing the reach of your church family.** No, I am not talking about just bringing in new members, although that is cool too. Find an agency, program, or ministry in your area that needs help, such as an

after-school program, a day care, or a poorly funded school. Partner with them by providing support, prayer, and volunteers. Adopt a "sister church" in a poverty-stricken country such as Africa or India. Provide financial resources, prayer, and mission teams to help spread the good news in another land.

(9) Pick a fight and get into "good trouble." Perhaps there is a social issue in the community where your church is located (and trust me, churches *everywhere* have social issues just outside their doors!). Become a champion for this social issue and help those in need who are affected by it. It may be high unemployment, illiteracy, drugs or alcohol, domestic violence, homelessness, or any of a host of other social ills. Become knowledgeable about the issues and do whatever you can to raise awareness and address it.

(10) Invest time to find out what your local community needs. Often churches offer worship services or ministry activities that do not address the real needs of their surrounding community. Much of what we do in the church is geared for the insiders. Recruit a few friends and do a community survey, either in person or through a mailing. Find out what the key concerns and predominate needs are around your church. Ask God to open your eyes to see where he is already at work around your church, and then develop ways to partner with him in addressing needs and offering hope.

One final word: if you are serious about becoming a New Testament church, be prepared for the kickback, negativity, and venom from those in your church who do not want to change. Persecution always follows anything worthwhile for the kingdom.

Jesus told us, *"If you belonged to the world, it would love you as its own. As it is, you do not belong to the world, but I have chosen you out of the world. That is why the world hates you. Remember what I told you: 'A servant is not greater than his master.' If they persecuted me, they will persecute you also. If they obeyed my teaching, they will obey yours also. They will treat you this way because of my name, for they do not know the one who sent me"* (John 1:19-21). Some people in your church do not want to have their comforts and entitlements challenged. They are self-centered and believe the church exists to serve their own needs. Some are just there because it is what is expected, or so they can include it on their civic resume. Others are simply spoiling for a fight.

Friendships will be stretched and challenged. Family relationships may be broken. Jesus said, *"Do not suppose that I have come to bring peace to the earth. I did not come to bring peace, but a sword. For I have come to turn 'a man against his father, a daughter against her mother, a daughter-in-law against her mother-in-law – a man's enemies will be the members of his own household'"* (Matthew 10:34-36).

The cost of choosing to follow Jesus is high. If we are willing to pay this price in the church, some of our relationships will be challenged, and quite likely changed in some way. In a previous appointment, as we went through a turnaround, one of the oldest families in the church was divided. Several family members wanted to see their church grow and move forward; others wanted it to say just like it had for decades. Eventually, several of the family members transferred to another church in the area.

Difficult? You bet.

Uncomfortable? Absolutely.

Necessary? Yes, according to God's plan and vision for that church. Those who left refused to see what God wanted to do in the church. They thought God would always keep their church the way it had been all their lives.

Turning a church around is extremely hard. It takes time, committed leaders, a strong pastoral presence, prayer, and a God-given vision. The majority of churches in the West are in need of transformation and turnaround. So there is definitely a need for courageous, Spirit-led believers to step up and re-capture the essence of the Christian movement. But it will not be easy, nor will it come quickly. Depending on the health of your church, along with other factors, a turnaround can take anywhere from four to eight years. You need to be committed to this for the long haul.

And if you are...

If the pastor and key church leaders are willing to follow Jesus obediently and completely, regardless of the personal or professional cost, then your church can regain the essence and spirit of Acts. God is waiting for churches to rise up, throw off the chains of institutionalism, and live in the Spirit. His heart for the lost has not changed; his yearning to be reconciled to all his creation is the same as it has ever been. He is simply waiting for individuals and churches that are willing to risk *everything* in order to glorify him and draw people to Christ.

It is time to get dangerous. It is time "*...to walk by faith, not by sight*" (2 Corinthians 5:7). It is time to "*...turn the world up-side down*" (Acts 17:6) once again. May God bless you, protect you, strengthen you, and guide you as you step out in faith, carrying on the mission of Jesus!

If you have experiences of how your church has responded to change and transformation; if you are part of a movement to return to the biblical model of the church; if your small group, class, or church are taking significant risks that challenge the status quo of the institutional church, I would love to hear from you. Please send your stories to:

revjtodd@yahoo.com.

If the material in this book has got you thinking in new and radical ways, you may also consider visiting my blog, Dreams Along The Way, which contains additional ideas and thoughts about the church, faith, and discipleship. You can find it at: **www.dreamsalongtheway.blogspot.com**.

Bibliography

Easum, William M. *Leadership on the Other Side* (Abingdon Press; Nashville, TN; 2000)

Hunter III, George G. *Radical Outreach: The Recovery Of Apostolic Ministry & Evangelism* (Abingdon Press; Nashville, TN; 2003)

Viola, Frank and Barna, George. *Pagan Christianity? Exploring the Roots of Our Church Practices* (Barna Books/ Tyndale House Publishing, 2008)

Webster's New Collegiate Dictionary (G. & C. Merriam Co., 1980)

RECOMMENDED READING
If you would like to learn more about things you have encountered in this devotional, please consider any of the following books.

Early church
Cahill, Thomas. *Desire of the Everlasting Hills: The World Before and After Jesus* (Nan A. Talese/Doubleday; New York, NY; 1999)

Hinson, E. Glenn. *The Early Church: Origins to the Dawn of the Middle Ages* (Abingdon Press; Nashville, TN; 1996)

MacCulloch, Diarmaid. *Christianity: The First Three Thousand Years* (Viking Press; New York, NY; 2009)

McKinion, Steven A. *Life and Practice in the Early Church: A Documentary Reader* (New York University Press; New York, NY; 2001)

Snyder, Howard A. *The Community of the King* (Inter-Varsity Press; Downer Grove, IL; 1977)

Viola, Frank. *Reimagining Church* (David C. Cook; Colorado Springs, CO; 2008)

Evangelism
Covell, Jim & Karen; Rogers, Victorya Michaels. *How To Talk About Jesus Without Freaking Out* (Multnomah Publishers; Sisters, OR; 2000)

Kallenberg, Brad. *Live To Tell: Evangelism For a Postmodern Age* (Brazos Press; Grand Rapids, MI; 2002)

Richardson, Rick. *Evangelism Outside the Box: New Ways to Help People Experience the Good News* (InterVarsity Press; Downers Grove, IL; 2000)

Webber, Robert E. *Ancient-Future Evangelism: Making Your Church a Faith-Forming Community* (Baker Books; Grand Rapids, MI; 2003)

Leadership

Beckham, William A. *The Second Reformation: Reshaping the Church for the 21ˢᵗ Century* (TOUCH Publications; Houston, TX; 1997)

Bullard, Jr., George. *Pursuing the Full Kingdom Potential of Your Congregation* (Chalice Press; St. Louis, MO; 2005)

Easum, William M. *Sacred Cows Make Gourmet Burgers: Ministry Anytime Anywhere by Anyone* (Abingdon Press; Nashville, TN; 1995)

Easum, William M. *A Second Resurrection: Leading Your Congregation To New Life* (Abingdon Press; Nashville, TN; 2007)

Foss, Michael W. *From Members To Disciples: Leadership Lessons From the Book of Acts* (Abingdon Press, Nashville; 2007)

Hunter III, George G. *The Apostolic Congregation: Church Growth Reconceived for a New Generation* (Abingdon Press; Nashville, TN; 2009)

McNeal, Reggie. *The Present Future: Six Tough Questions for the Church* (Jossey Bass; San Francisco, CA; 2003)

McNeal, Reggie. *Missional Renaissance: Changing the Scorecard For the Church* (Jossey-Bass; San Francisco, CA; 2009)

Schnase, Robert. *Five Practices of Fruitful Congregations* (Abingdon Press; Nashville, TN; 2007)

Slaughter, Michael. *Unlearning Church: Just When You Thought You Had Leadership All Figured Out* (GROUP Publishing; Loveland, CO; 2002)

Sweet, Leonard. *AquaChurch: Essential Leadership Arts for Piloting Your Church in Today's Fluid Culture* (GROUP Publishing; Loveland, CO; 1999)

Lay-led ministry

Ogden, Greg. *The New Reformation: Returning the Ministry to the People of God* (Zondervan; Grand Rapids, MI; 1990)

Steinbron, Melvin J. *The Lay Driven Church: How To Empower the People in Your Church To Share the Tasks of Ministry* (Regal Books; Ventura, CA; 1997)

Missions/outreach

Easum, William M. *Unfreezing Moves: Following Jesus Into the Mission Field* (Abingdon Press; Nashville, TN; 2001)

Frost, Michael and Alan Hirsch. *ReJesus: A Wild Messiah for a Missional Church* (Hendrickson Publishing; Peabody, MA; 2009)

Hirsch, Alan. *The Forgotten Ways: Reactivating the Missional Church* (Brazos Press; Grand Rapids, MI; 2006)

Platt, David. *Radical Together: Unleashing the People of God For the Purpose of God* (Multnomah Books; Colorado Springs, CO; 2011)

Postmodernism/culture
Clapp, Rodney. *A Peculiar People: The Church As Culture in a Post-Christian Society* (InterVarsity Press; Downers Grove, IL; 1996)

Gibbs, Eddie and Ryan K. Bolger. *Emerging Churches: Creating Christian Community in Postmodern Cultures* (Baker Academic; Grand Rapids, MI; 2005)

Kinnaman, David. *UnChristian: What a New Generation Really Thinks About Christianity... And Why It Matters* (Baker Books; Grand Rapids, MI; 2007)

Platt, David. *Radical: Taking Back Your Faith from the American Dream* (Multnomah Press; Colorado Springs, CO; 2010)

Smith, Jr., Chuck. *The End of the World... As We Know It* (Waterbrook Press; Colorado Springs, CO; 2001)

Sweet, Leonard. *Postmodern Pilgrims: First Century Passion For the 21st Century World* (Broadman & Holman Publishers; Nashville, TN; 2000)

Made in the USA
Lexington, KY
03 November 2013